SMOKE UP THE RIVER

Also by Van Hawkins

Hampton and Newport News
A look at two historic Virginia towns

Dorothy and the Shipbuilders of Newport News
The story of an iconic American shipyard

The Historic Triangle
How Jamestown, Williamsburg, and
Yorktown made American history

Plowing New Ground
The Southern Tenant Farmers Union
and its place in Delta history

Duty Bound
The Hyatt brothers and Confederates
of the Third Arkansas Infantry Regiment

Horizons
A novel

A New Deal in Dyess
The Depression Era
Agricultural Resettlement Colony in Arkansas

SMOKE UP THE RIVER

Steamboats and the Arkansas Delta

By Van Hawkins

Smoke Up the River
Steamboats and the Arkansas Delta

Book designed by Mary Reed Melton

Printed in the United States of America
First Printing 2016

ISBN: 978-0-9863992-1-3

Library of Congress Control Number: 2016910668

Writers Bloc
Jonesboro, Arkansas

For Ruth

Table of Contents

Appendices

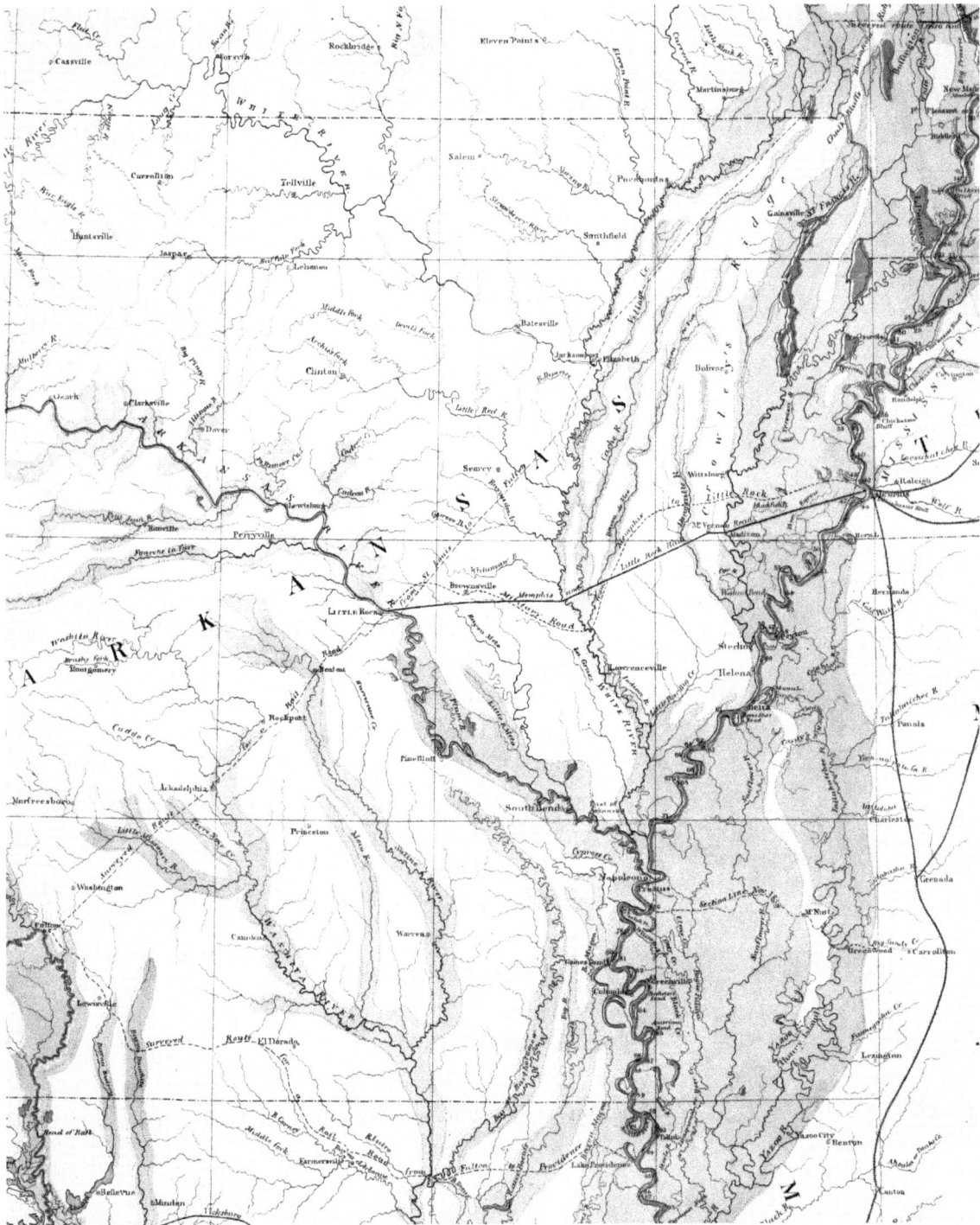

Arkansas segment of an 1861 map of the Mississippi River alluvial region. Created by
the United States Army Corp of Topographical Engineers. Library of Congress.

Notes and Acknowledgements

The Mississippi River is said to run fast and deep. This book shares one characteristic, but not the other. It is not a study of steamboats in great depth, from the diameter of smokestacks on each vessel to the maximum pressure tolerated by various boilers. Rather, it is designed to provide an easily accessible overview of steamboats that in one way or another had ties to what is called the Arkansas Delta. Brief commentary about individual boats is included as well as historic context when a noteworthy one exists. Sections include river craft prior to the advent of steamboats, antebellum boats, Civil War vessels, and post-war steamers from 1865 to 1899. The story ends with the century, a somewhat arbitrary conclusion, but railroads and other means of transportation and shipping dominated by then. By 1900, riverboats usually picked up and delivered cargo at towns and commercial centers and not at plantation landings. An era had ended, one that "perfectly expressed America," according to author Bernard DeVoto.[1]

Most information concerning the 1870s comes from typed pages in several binders compiled by William H. Tippitt and located at the Phillips County Library in Helena-West Helena, Arkansas. A former river pilot and newspaper columnist, Tippitt became an informal authority on river matters. He admits in introductory comments from April 1967 that his spelling is "atrocious," and he "abhors" proof reading. These are true. Additionally, attribution sometimes is as muddy as the big river or not included at all. Due to concerns about structure, coherence, and length, material herein is sometimes edited, but with original

intent maintained. Tippitt's compendium itemizes steamers built, destroyed, or noteworthy during the 1870s. Citations direct readers to his manuscript pages and to other sources as well. Frequently used resources for boat lists are identified by author and page number. Coverage of the 1870s is longer than other periods due to the volume of material. Authors Joan W. Gandy and Thomas H. Gandy provide another reason for concentration on this era. "While praise for the extravagance and beauty of pre-Civil War boats fills volumes, the fact is that the boats of the postwar years were by necessity superior."[2]

Other key resources include *Way's Packet Directory, 1848-1994; Lloyd's Steamboat Directory and Disasters on the Western Waters; Fifty years on the Mississippi or Gould's History of River Navigation,* and *Steamboats and Ferries on the White River: A Heritage Revisited.* In instances where sources provide different versions of events, each is included without an attempt to referee unless a clear winner is evident. Though the focus of this book is on the Arkansas Delta, hereafter called the Delta, some exceptions are made. Locations such as Little Rock, Arkansas are included when central to the story though technically beyond this book's geographic scope. Some ongoing peculiarities deserve mention. Tellers of riverboat tales tended to take liberties with spelling, such as the frequent merging of two words into one — "wharfboat" for example. They are allowed this privilege in order to keep usages consistent throughout. When possible and appropriate, the year of a boat's construction, usually the year of first documentation, follows its

---

[1]Bernard DeVoto, *Mark Twain's America* (New York: Cambridge, 1951), 106. DeVoto covers the history of this American writer and social forces that helped create his art and a country on the move. Twain's experiences included work as a printer, silver miner, riverboat pilot, and writer. The melding of his riverboat observations and imagination produced remarkable literature.

[2]Joan W. Gandy and Thomas H. Gandy, *The Mississippi Steamboat Era in Historic Photographs, Natchez to New Orleans 1870-1920.* (Mineola, NY: Dover Publications, 1987), 68. The authors have produced a richly illustrated book comprised of photos by Henry Norman and Henry Gurney along with brief commentary. At first Gurney's assistant, Norman eventually set out on his own and for 30 years created a visual history of Natchez and related topics.

name in parenthesis. Popular boat names might appear on several different vessels, but only those with Arkansas connections are included. Finally, readers should keep in mind that with respect to the rivers, particularly the Mississippi, what was true one day may not have been the next. "Old Man River" stayed hungry, constantly devouring chunks of land to whet his appetite.

Many people helped with this book. Lindsey Tosh sorted through the Tippitt material and helped compile his information. Several authorities on subjects herein were kind enough to read the manuscript and offer valuable suggestions: Dr. Michael B. Dougan, Distinguished Professor of History Emeritus at Arkansas State University; Charles Bogart, Western Rivers Columnist, *PowerShips*, Steamboat Historical Society of America; and Allison Hiblong, Director of Operations, Arkansas Inland Maritime Museum. Mary Reed Melton's design skills gave organization to the book. My wife Ruth deserves enormous credit for her astute editing. Her skills continue to amaze me, and she never runs out of steam.

Terminology

The following terms are used in this story, and some may be unfamiliar to general readers. Though not exhaustive, these definitions should limit trips to a dictionary or encyclopedia.

Aft: Rear section of a boat.

Bales: Cotton bales consist of about 500 pounds of lint without seed compressed into oblong blocks held in place by netting. The season for transporting bales by boat usually began in September, when many small steamers picked them up at Delta towns and landings on Lower Mississippi River tributaries. Shallow draft vessels transported cotton to major collection points such as Memphis, where larger steamers took over and usually headed to New Orleans.

Bar: Sedimentary shoal formed in navigable waters where the current slows down. The many varieties include rock bars, gravel bars, and sand bars, the most common form. They could be hidden beneath water or observable, temporary or permanent. All endangered river traffic.

Barge: Considered to belong in the keelboat classification, but early barges usually had no cover for shelter. A frame covered with planking, barges were longer, wider, and heavier than regular keelboats.

Barques: Small vessels propelled by sail or oars.

Beacons: Lights located on rivers or along them to aid navigators.

Boneyard: Where dilapidated steamboats were scrapped.

Bell boats: Boats containing a diving bell that enabled salvagers to descend to the bottom of a river to retrieve property and materials from sunken riverboats. James B. Eads developed the diving bell after working on a steamboat and noting enormous boat losses. Eads started a successful salvage business in 1842 utilizing a series of bell boats bearing the name *Submarine*. Salvagers usually received a percentage of the property value saved, ranging from 20 to 75 percent.[3]

Bills of lading: Receipts issued by a carrier for cargo to be transported.

Boilers: Enclosed tubes in which water was heated to supply steam driving an engine.

Bendways: Lateral bends or meanders of the river created through erosion of the banks outside of the curves and sediment deposits on the banks inside of the curves. Notable historic bends along the Arkansas stretch of the Mississippi River included Barfield, Nodena, Council, Old Town, Concordia, Scrubgrass, Victoria, Cypress, Chowtaw, Yellow, Walker, and Kentucky bends.

Bow: Foremost part of a vessel.

Breaks: Points of discontinuity between two levels of a ship's deck.

Bulkhead: The wall in a boat.

Cabins: Compartments that offered accommodations and facilities for passengers and crews; also a private room on a passenger ship. Author Louis C. Hunter describes cabin space in more elaborate steamers. It typically consisted of "a long and narrow saloon

---

[3]Louis C. Hunter, *Steamboats on the Western Rivers. An Economic and Technological History* (New York: Dover Publications, 1949), 119. Hunter's book covers most aspects of steamboat development and operation on western rivers, including construction, equipment, steamboat life, economics, hazards and risks, competition, and ultimate decline of the industry.

flanked on each side by a row of staterooms. At the forward end of the saloon on either side in line with staterooms were the clerk's office and the bar. Before the introduction of the texas [deck] the quarters of the captain and pilots as well as the clerk were usually located in the forward part of the cabin." Washrooms, barbershop, nursery, pantry, kitchen, and various service rooms usually were on either side of the cabin deck. Most staterooms had doors that accessed the outside gallery as well as the saloon.[4]

Capstan: Drum that rotates, around which a hauling line is wrapped several times for the purpose of lifting heavy weights such as anchors.

Catfish Navy: Riverboats that delivered supplies to the Gulf of Mexico.

Cave-in: When the banks of a river give way under natural forces. Author Thomas Foti explains how the caving in of a shoreline comes about: "Geologists say that meandering is a way for rivers to rid themselves of excess energy. In essence, the water at any given point is being pushed by faster-moving water from above into slower-moving water below. Where's the water to go except sideways? How, then, does the river spend that excess energy? In caving and carving the bank on the outsides of bends, and in depositing new land on the insides of the bends."[5]

Channel: The deeper part of a river. When riverbeds are formed by sand a channel often shifts in response to the volume and velocity of water. With other bottom formations, such as gravel or rock, channels tend to hold their position from year to year.

Chutes: Narrow channels with an exceptionally rapid current.

Clerk: A boat's head clerk served as business manager, freight solicitor, and passenger host.

Combine: Consortium of boat owners formed to maintain profitable prices. They usually developed after cutthroat competition among steamers led to financial losses. Though these organizations dated from the 1820s, they became common after the Civil War.

Cordelling: Flatboat crews used lines tied to trees ashore to pull the vessel along.

Cottonclads: Wooden vessels used during the Civil War primarily for riverine service. Their sides were lined with cotton bales for protection from small arms fire.

Doctor: Auxiliary engine that cured several mechanical problems. It operated a pump for supplying engine water, bilge pumps, and was used to fire up engines.

Doldrums: State of inactivity.

Draft: Depth of a vessel from waterline to keel.

Dunnage: Materials placed under or among goods carried as cargo in the hold of a vessel to keep freight from motion and harm.

Eddy: Whirlpool or countercurrent alongside the main flow of water.

Elevators: Though not exclusively used by riverboats, these structures became central to freight shipment. They provided cargo storage and served as central shipping points. Elevators sometimes became a focal point of protests by dock workers who unloaded riverboats. Large vessels with a full cargo needed from 50 to 75 men to load and unload them. Using about 15 men, elevators could perform the same task in half the time.

---

[4]Hunter, 394.

[5]Thomas Foti, "The River's Gifts and Curses," *The Arkansas Delta. Land of Paradox*, edited by Jeannie Whayne and Willard B. Gatewood (Fayetteville: University of Arkansas Press, 1993), 31. This collection of essays focuses on the so-called Arkansas Delta. The book's wide-ranging points of view cover European exploration, the colonial era, Civil War years, and beyond. In the journey, cultural and business developments along with personal stories provide an understanding of what happened on the way.

Mississippi River Cutoffs

Cutoffs were new channels cut out of land between river bends, thus significantly shortening the river over time. According to authors Charles A. Camillo and Matthew T. Pearcy, "Prior to settlement of the lower Mississippi Valley, cutoffs occurred in the river at a rate 13 to 15 in the course of a century, with 15 recorded cutoffs occurring between 1722 and 1884, and probably many more going unrecorded." The Mississippi River Commission worked to end this phenomenon, indicating that its "first duty to navigation and flood control was to prevent cutoffs."[6]

In Mark Twain's View

In his inimitable fashion, Twain debunks attempts to measure the Mississippi River, announcing that "In the space of one hundred and seventy-six years the Lower Mississippi has shortened itself two hundred and forty-two miles. That is an average of a trifle over one mile and a third per year. Therefore, any calm person, who is not blind or idiotic, can see that in the Old Oolitic Silurian [sic] Period, just a million years ago next November, the Lower Mississippi River was upwards of one million three hundred thousand miles long, and stuck out over the Gulf of Mexico like a fishing rod. And by the same token any person can see that seven hundred and forty-two years from now the Lower Mississippi will be only a mile and three quarters long, and Cairo and New Orleans will have joined their streets together, and be plodding comfortably along under a single mayor and a mutual board of aldermen. There is something fascinating about science. One gets such wholesale returns of conjecture out of such a trifling investment of fact."[7]

Mark Twain aboard a steamer. From *Mark Twain. An Illustrated Biography*, title page.

---

[6]Charles A. Camillo and Matthew T. Pearcy, *Upon Their Shoulders. A history of the Mississippi River Commission from its inception through the advent of the modern Mississippi River and Tributaries Project* (Vicksburg: Mississippi River Commission, 2006), 187. The commission was formed in August 1879 and consisted of seven men appointed by President Rutherford B. Hayes. Six were civil engineers and the seventh an attorney. They were tasked with making the river a safe commercial artery and protecting adjacent lands from overflows.

[7]Mark Twain, *Life on the Mississippi* (New York: Signet Classic, 2001), 106. As his evaluation of the Mississippi River's length suggests, Twain's take on such things can be hilarious. This volume connects the big river's history and the writer's experiences on it as a riverboat pilot and traveler. One can perceive in his anecdotes and observations the source material for classics such as *Adventures of Huckleberry Finn*.

Ferries

Since many waterways traverse the Delta, relatively small and flat wooden ferries became a means to get from one side of a river to the other. Operators had to pole or pull the ferry across a river using heavy rope. Men ashore would pull, and those aboard would pole. County courts determined the amount of fees that could be charged by ferries, and the following schedule provides the cost of crossing the White River during 1865.

- Four-wheel wagon drawn by one to four horses or mules, .75 to 1.00
- Four-wheel wagon drawn by five or six horses, 1.10 to 1.20
- One man on foot or horse, .10 to .25
- One loose horse or other stock by head, .10
- Freight, lbs not stated, 1.00[8]

Flatboat: Craft shaped like a rectangular box constructed of planks generally 100 feet long and steered with oars or sweeps.

Float barges: Shippers began sending coal to the Lower Mississippi in about 1835 by using float barges. These craft measured approximately 150 feet wide and 150 feet long and held about 10,000 bushels of coal. Often lashed in pairs, each barge contained a crew consisting of two pilots, a cook, and six men at the sweeps or oars. Owners usually broke up the craft and sold the wood at journey's end.

Flue: Shaft through which steam escapes.

Flumes: Deep, narrow channels or ravines with a stream running through them.

Fly Time: Period between planting crops and harvesting them. A term primarily used on the Lower Mississippi.

Fore: Toward the front of a ship.

Hog chain: Long chain stretching from bow to stern on vessels to keep them from bowing up in the middle and sagging at the ends.

Hold: Below-deck area of the vessel usually used for carrying cargo.

Horns: "She takes the horns" is an old Mississippi River expression. The fastest boats displayed gilded deer antlers. Sometimes these coveted trophies appeared on the hurricane roof and other times on the pilothouse.[9]

Hurricane: Deck at or near the top of a boat's superstructure.

Islands: Mississippi islands below the mouth of the Ohio River have been numbered, but numbers can be irregular since the river constantly creates and eliminates islands. Formation of a new island is called "growing up," and it occurs where alluvial soil builds up.[10]

---

[8] Michael Krivor and Andrew Buchner, *Cultural Resources Reconnaissance Study of the White River Navigation Project.* Final Report, Vol. I. Prepared for Army Corps of Engineers Memphis District, Memphis, Tennessee (Panamerican Consultants Inc.: April 2001), 82. Hereafter cited as Krivor. This report covers 245 river miles of the Lower White River. It focuses on such matters as navigation history, archaeological efforts, historic properties, and cultural resources.

[9] Frederick Way, Jr., *She Takes the Horns. Steamboat Racing on the Western Waters* (Cincinnati: Young and Klein, 1953), 9. Way was arguably the chief authority on American steamboats for many years. He grew up near the Ohio River and became infatuated with river men and their steamers. In 1914, when he was only 13 years old, Way began preparing steamboat histories. He attended the University of Cincinnati for one year before choosing a life on the river. Way earned a pilot's license, a master designation, and operated the packet *Betsy Ann* for several years. He published extensively on river matters, including seven books, and edited a river history journal. In 1989 Way was named Nathaniel Bowditch Maritime Scholar of the Year by the American Merchant Marine Museum. He died in 1992.

[10] John Francis McDermott, editor, *Before Mark Twain: A Sampler of Old, Old Times on the Mississippi* (Carbondale: Southern Illinois University Press, 1968), 131-132. The author tells stories collected from a variety of sources to depict life on the Mississippi River before Mark Twain took up pen and paper. These tales, some tall, some short, cover the gamut of people and experiences. There are stoic captains and crooked gamblers, southern belles and slaves. All appear amid the delights and difficulties of life on the river.

Jackstaff: Flagpole.

Johnboat: Homemade craft with square ends often constructed with wide planks.

Keelboat: Long, narrow riverboat with pointed ends. Built from wood, it often measured 80 feet long and 18 feet wide. The vessel would be poled, towed from the bank, rowed, or sailed.

Larboard: Side of a vessel where cargo is loaded.

Lighter: Long, narrow craft used to lighten the load of a bigger vessel. Cargo would be transferred until the steamboat was lightened sufficiently to free it from a bar or other impediment. Big boats reloaded the cargo after reaching deeper water.

Market Boats: Craft going downriver to barter and sell goods to farmers and planters.

Mark twain: The famous writer, Samuel L. Clemens, took his pen name from steamer jargon. Boats measured depth by using lead lines. When the line heaved off the bow marked water 12 feet deep, it was known as safe water, or mark twain.

Model barge: A vessel constructed by using a wooden model.

Mosquito Fleet: Small steamers on the Lower Ohio or its tributaries.

Oxbow lake: An oxbow lake is created when the river cuts through the narrow end of a bend, separating the bend from the main channel. The area between the main channel and the bend then begins to fill in with alluvial soil, eventually leaving the former bend as a u-shaped or oxbow-shaped separate lake.

Packets: Boats carrying mail, freight, and people regularly on a fixed route. As river commerce increased, so did the need for regularity and reliability of service. Thus packets soon replaced transient vessels. Packet lines typically consisted of two or more boats providing service in a specific trade. They became particularly important in local trades and shorter distances, especially in routes that joined tributaries with trunk lines in a river system. According to Hunter, those vessels "customarily arranged to provide daily, thrice-weekly, semiweekly, or weekly departures in each direction."[11] Dependable schedules allowed packets to charge higher rates and develop reliable business relationships with shippers.

Pilot: Person who guides the course of a vessel.

Pilot's License. Duane Huddleston Collection, Original in the Mariner's Museum, Newport News, Virginia.

---

[11]Hunter, 321.

Pirogue: Long, narrow canoe made from a single tree trunk.

Porter: Though not exclusively working on steamboats, porters assisted passengers by carrying luggage on and off the vessel. A Memphis *Avalanche* on October 18, 1876, reported a controversy regarding their compensation. "The question of whether or not to pay the porters on steamboats [rather than having them work for tips] has come up again. It is argued that if paid, the porters will not be as zealous as they now are, will not be as attentive to the wants of the passengers, will not guard their baggage as carefully as they do now, and that the boat would lose much time at the various landings while porters hunted for passengers' luggage in the baggage room. There has been considerable complaint at the charges made by some porters on our boats in regards to handling of passenger baggage. It is true that the porter is furnished his meals free of charge and given a place to sleep in the baggage room, but his earnings depend upon the generosity of the public. At times not too generous."

Raft: A small watercraft, but on western rivers it meant something else as well. It referred to a major floating accumulation of snags, logs, trees, and other materials that could obstruct the river for miles. Whether one continuous mass or a series of obstructions, such rafts could make river traffic difficult to impossible.

Rivers and Harbors Act: Passed by the U. S. Congress in 1890, this legislation provided for a rapid increase of levee construction to prevent or minimize periodic flooding in the Lower Mississippi Delta.

Rousters: Also roustabouts. Men who worked on wharves, usually Irish or German prior to the Civil War. After the war many black workers filled the slots.

Sandbars: A constant hazard of navigation. Long sandbars were known as reefs. Ripples and shoals existed where sandbars came in quick succession.

Sawyer: Snag making an up and down motion in the water.

Scaping out: Opening a vessel's safety valves to release steam and avoid an unsafe build-up of pressure.

Sidewheelers: Vessels with paddle wheels located at the side. Author Leslie C. Stewart-Abernathy describes this design's advantages. "During the antebellum golden age of steam-boating, the side-wheelers had the glory. A side-wheeler was faster and more maneuverable, since increasing power to one side or the other made turning much easier. There was also less vibration with the engines next to the paddle wheels, and passengers did not like vibration."[12]

Snag: Usually driftwood or trees below the surface that when struck might damage the vessel.

Snagboat: Boat that removes snags from rivers.

Sparring: A technique used to free a grounded boat; also called "grasshoppering" or "walking the boat." Spars were poles set in the ground ahead of the vessel with the upper end overhanging the forecastle. Using leverage, the crew lifted up the craft and shoved it off an impediment.

Stacks: Smokestacks.

Stage: Gangplank.

Starboard: Right side of a vessel when one is facing forward.

Stern: Rearmost part of a boat.

---

[12]Leslie C. Stewart-Abernathy, editor, *Ghost Boats on the Mississippi: Discovering Our Working Past* (Fayetteville: Arkansas Archeological Survey, University of Arkansas System, 2002), 50. Stewart-Abernathy's book is a detailed study of Mississippi riverboat wrecks recovered by archaeologists.

Sternwheelers: Steamers with paddles on the boat's stern. Stewart-Abernathy says that this boat design dominated after the 1880s for several reasons, including "improvements in design and engineering. Beneficial modifications included mounting the paddle wheel to occupy the full width of the vessel's stern, improvements in the transfer of power from engine to wheel, and perfection of the balance rudder." These steamers "actually steered better going backward than forward. This was a great advantage at the many locations on the rivers where there were bow-on landings, but no dock facilities."[13]

Swamp: When water pours over the side of a boat.

Texas: Owners named cabins for various states and designated a large one on the upper deck the texas. Even after this practice ended, the cabin area for the crew on the upper deck remained the texas.

Tinclads: Lightly armored steamers turned into gunboats during the Civil War. Thin iron plating allowed them to patrol in shallow waters.

Trades: Steamboats generally worked specific routes called trades, such as White River-Memphis trade. Small boats running between nearby locations were called short traders.

Tributary: Stream of water flowing into a larger body of water.

Trip: A boat's freight was called a trip, a trip of cotton for example, but it also referred to a journey.

Western steamboats: Steamers generally came in two versions, eastern or western. Western vessels that plied the Mississippi River and Delta tributaries evolved from oceangoing designs into riverine craft. Their hull lost depth, keels disappeared, and the superstructure rose.

Wharfboat: Moored boat used as a wharf on the side of a riverbank.

Whistles: Steamboats announced their arrivals and departures with whistles. Each vessel produced a distinct sound according to the number of tubes and their sizes. Boats typically sported one to five tubes that could be blown separately or all together, depending on the signal desired. An article in the Memphis *Commercial Appeal* dated October 9, 1943, described an unusual signal. "Fine bells and whistles used to be as essential to old time river packets as engines and boilers. Owners of boats seldom brought out a new one that wasn't equipped with a mellow sounding whistle or a musically toned bell. When the Cincinnati and New Orleans packet *Will Kyle* was built she was given a wildcat whistle, one with a sound like the scream of a panther. On her first trip down the Ohio River, the whistle almost frightened people into fits. Many believed it was a wild animal. Armed men went into the timber searching for it before someone discovered it was the *Kyle's* whistle." In order to prevent "fits" on the part of their citizens, some city councils passed ordinances prohibiting boats from sounding their whistles in port.

Wooding: Process of stopping a steamboat at certain places along the river where wood could be purchased to fuel the boat's boilers.

Yawl: Small boat that belongs to a larger vessel.

---

[13]Stewart-Abernathy, 52.

Wharfboats such as this one at Natchez, Mississippi allowed transfer of cargo to and from vessels. Louisiana State University Libraries, Special Collections, Thomas H. and Joan W. Gandy Photograph Collection. Wharfboats also provided entertainment of a sordid sort for boat crews and male passengers. Temptations included gambling, drinking, and bawdy pursuits. During the 1870s some upstanding Memphis citizens sought to have wharfboats removed from the levee, thus eliminating opportunities for river men to blow off steam. The indignant Memphians failed in this endeavor, but succeeded in limiting wharfboat activities to handling freight and not vices.[14]

---

[14]Tippitt, 1870, 13.

Rivers that Run Through It

Complexities abound when considering the Mississippi Delta, beginning with the fact that it is not a delta. It can be described as a "deep river valley filled with layers of sediments that have produced a broad, sinuous, flat floodplain."[15] The alluvial floodplain known as the Lower Mississippi stretches from Cairo, Illinois to the Gulf of Mexico. The Mississippi Delta is further distinguished by its east and west sides. This book focuses on the west side, where Arkansas hugs the big river.

Many rivers flow through Arkansas, but its two major ones are the Arkansas and the White. The Arkansas River begins in Colorado and becomes Arkansas's prominent waterway to the Mississippi River. Recorded exploration of this river by Europeans began when Hernando de Soto ascended it during the 1540s. Jean-Baptiste Bénard de la Harpe came in December 1722 on what was to be one of several searches for riches, including an emerald rock supposedly located upriver. According to author Owen Lyon, after roughly 30 days of poling and rowing, 22 soldiers and three Native Americans found a big rock, but no emerald. The location came to be known as Big Rock, and is not far from a smaller stone promontory below and across the river called Little Rock.[16] Thomas Nuttall made a less ambitious trip on the river in 1819, and author Michael Dougan shares some negative impressions that Nuttall noted in a journal, including comments about the "'aborigines'" he discovered. Dougan observes that one can't be sure if Nuttall is referring to Native Americans or Arkansas settlers. Nuttall gives us a hint, writing that "it is to be regretted that the widely scattered state of the population of this territory is but too favorable to the spread of ignorance and barbarism."[17] Unfortunately for many travelers heading up the Arkansas River, they began at Napoleon, Arkansas near the river's mouth, not a favorable starting point. Dougan quotes Judge Peter Daniel, who called the town "the most wretched of wretched places."[18]

Another major conduit to the Mississippi River, the White begins near Fayetteville, Arkansas and winds its way east and south for about 720 miles before arriving at the Mississippi River about 70 miles south of Helena, Arkansas. The Lower White is considered by many to begin at Jacksonport, Arkansas. French traders made their way along this portion of the river as early as 1745, gathering items such as fur and buffalo meat for trade or sale. They named the river LaRiviere Blancho due to its clear water. Settlers followed the French, pushing out Native Americans from their land. The *Arkansas Gazette* on March 25, 1820, announced that "Strangers are arriving here almost daily, with the intention of exploring or settling in this country. Families and others are flooding in great numbers up the White River."

---

[15] Fiona Davidson and Tom Paradise, "Landscape, Environment, and Geography of the Mississippi River Delta Region," *Defining the Delta. Multidisciplinary Perspectives on the Lower Mississippi River Delta,* Janelle Collins, editor (Fayetteville: University of Arkansas Press, 2016), 65. This collection covers the Lower Mississippi Delta from many perspectives. Essays focus on diverse features such as geology, archaeology, history, politics, and others. From them a picture emerges of a cultural quilt with many colors.

[16] Owen Lyon, "The Quapaws and Little Rock," *Arkansas Historical Quarterly* 8:4 (Winter 1949), 338-339.

[17] Michael B. Dougan, *Arkansas Odyssey. The Saga of Arkansas From Prehistoric Times to Present* (Little Rock: Rose Publishing Company, Inc., 1994), 532. Dougan's book is both informative and a good read. He begins with Native Americans in Arkansas and continues through the promise and problems of modernization. Along the way the author covers major events, historic periods, and forces that contributed to the state's development.

[18] Dougan, 119.

This map created in 1836, the year Arkansas became a state, shows steamboat routes and distances to major shipping destinations.   Tanner Universal Atlas. Arkansas History Commission.

Before the Steamers

Native Americans and European trappers and traders used various means to travel along Delta waterways, such as canoes, pirogues, and flat-bottomed cypress dugouts. The region's many rivers made such transportation possible. Water in one form or another has traversed 51 of Arkansas's 75 counties, and the Mississippi River touches virtually all of the Arkansas Delta's eastern border. When commercial prospects called for carrying more goods and passengers, haulers developed flatboats and keelboats. Crews on those craft usually steered them with a stern oar and two oars at the bow. They had to pole their vessels against the current and in some cases pull the boat forward using ropes held by mates on the riverbank. In this manner, passage from New Orleans upriver to Louisville, Kentucky could take six months. That is why many riverboat owners sold their craft for wood after reaching southern destinations and began a long walk home using the Natchez Trace, a worn path infested with robbers and cutthroats.

During the first six months of 1801, freight arriving at New Orleans came in "450 flatboats, 26 keelboats, a brig, two schooners, and seven pirogues," according to author Hodding Carter.[19] In addition to cargo, many boats carried immigrants seeking a new home in the region. Authors E. L. Bogart and C. M. Thompson provide an observer's description of them. "Today we passed two large rafts lashed together. Several families were transporting themselves and their property to the land of promise in the western woods." Each of these rafts had a house on it and by "each house was a stack of hay around which horses and cows were feeding. Paraphernalia of a farm yard, including plows, pigs, wagons, children [an odd bit of farm paraphernalia], and poultry were carelessly distributed. The boat floats with the current to the place selected. On arrival they step ashore, build a hut from the timber of the boat, and commence business."[20]

Although immigrants had to overcome many of nature's barriers during the early 1800s, some failed to reach their destination after falling victim to villains. Many pirates who preyed on river shipping occupied Island No. 94, called the Crow's Nest, below the Arkansas-Louisiana state line. This location became a den of thieves and murderers. Its denizens stopped passing boats, stole the cargo, and murdered their crews. Author E. W. Gould says that in autumn 1809, men from several boats north of the Crow's Nest "were well informed as to the villainies of those who harbored on the little island a few miles below them. By what means it was brought about, or at whose suggestion or influence, it was never known. But one dark night, a few hours before daylight, eighty or ninety men from the wind-bound crafts, well-armed, descended in their small boats to the Crow's Nest and surprised its occupants, whom they secured after a short encounter, in which two of the boatmen were wounded and several of the robbers killed. Nineteen men, a boy of fifteen, and two women were thus captured." Shortly after sunrise, vigilantes freed the boy on account of his youth and the two women. "What was the punishment meted out to the men, whether shot or hanged, was never ascertained with any degree of certainty." Regardless, the brigands

---

[19]Hodding Carter, *Lower Mississippi* (New York: Rinehart & Company, 1942), 215. Carter's prolific writing about the South won for him the nickname, "Spokesman of the New South." In this book, Carter traces various historic eras along the Lower Mississississipi, beginning with Spanish exploration and going through Civil War, Reconstruction, and modern developments such as flood control.

[20]E. L. Bogart and C. M. Thompson, *Readings in the Economic History of the United States* (New York: Longmans, Green and Co., 1916), 352. In this prolific work, editors Bogart and Thompson note that their mission has been to supplement more systematic textbooks and records with materials from contemporary sources during each historic period. While official documents have been included, they are illuminated through firsthand accounts of travelers, observers, and others qualified to speak authoritatively.

were eliminated, and the 1811-1812 New Madrid earthquakes eliminated the island.[21] Despite such severe penalties inflicted on pirates by posses, the outlaw problem continued.

Though many haulers of goods and people preferred flatboats and keelboats, Delta rivers sported numerous makes and models of vessels during the early 1800s. Timothy Flint, whose travels led him along land that bordered the Mississippi River, describes heavy boat traffic along the Delta. While visiting New Madrid, Missouri, just above what became the Arkansas state line, he observed about 100 boats stopping over, many before heading downriver to the Arkansas Delta. Flint observed boats carrying "planks, from the pine forests of the southwest of New York. . . . From Kentucky, pork, flour, whiskey, hemp, tobacco, bagging, and bale-rope. From Tennessee there are the same articles, together with great quantities of cotton. From Missouri and Illinois, cattle and horses, the same articles generally from Ohio, together with peltry and lead from Missouri. Some boats are loaded with corn in the ear and in bulk; others with barrels of apples and potatoes. Some have loads of cider, and what they call 'cider royal' or cider that has been strengthened by boiling or freezing. There are dried fruits, every kind of spirits manufactured in these regions, and in short, the products of the ingenuity and agriculture of the whole upper country of the west."[22]

In another letter to his brother, Flint describes land surrounding rivers and why it made water travel a necessity. "There are immense swamps of cypress, which swamps constitute a vast proportion of the inundated lands of the Mississippi [River] and its waters. No prospect on earth can be more gloomy. . . . A cypress swamp, with its countless interlaced branches of a hoary grey, has an aspect of desolation and death that, often as I have been impressed with it, I cannot describe. . . . The water in which they grow is a vast and dead level, two or three feet deep, still leaving the innumerable cypress "knees," as they are called . . . throwing their points above the waters."[23] To avoid such imposing terrain, many shippers and travelers chose rivers. Unfortunately, some business trips down the Mississippi River ended in disasters.

Davy Crockett experienced one such disaster and describes it in his purported autobiography. The famous frontiersman loaded about 30,000 wooden staves on two boats and headed toward New Orleans. When his crews reached the Mississippi River he found that "all my hands were bad scared and in fact I believe I was scared a little the worst of any; for I had never been down the river and I soon discovered that my pilot was as ignorant of the business as myself." When Crockett went below deck to warm himself the vessel began "floating sideways. The first thing I know'd after this we went broadside full tilt against the head of an island where a large raft of drift timber had lodged. The nature of such a place would be, as everybody knows, to suck the boats down and turn them right under this raft; and the uppermost boat would, of course, be suck'd down and go under first. As soon as we struck, I bulged [sic] for my hatchway as the boat was turning under sure enough." However, water pouring into the hatch blocked his exit, so

[21]E. W. Gould, *Fifty Years on the Mississippi or Gould's History of River Navigation* (Columbus, Ohio: Long's College Book Company, 1951), 58-59. Gould spells out the content of his book early on. It includes navigation of western rivers before the introduction of steam—-character of the early navigators—-description of first steamboats—- their effect upon the settlement of the Valley of the Mississippi—-character and speed of boats at different periods—-appropriations by Congress for the improvement of western water ways—-floods in the Mississippi Valley for 150 years and much more.

[22]Timothy Flint, *Recollections of the last Ten Years, Passed in Occasional Residences and Journeyings in the Valley of the Mississippi, from Pittsburgh and the Missouri to the Gulf of Mexico, and from Florida to the Spanish Frontier: In a series of Letters to the Rev. James Flint, of Salem, Massachusetts* (Boston: Cunnings, Hilliard, 1826), 103. Flint was a Presbyterian minister from New England who traveled extensively as a missionary in the Mississippi River Valley. Extensive writings about his travels made him an important man of letters in the American West during the first half of the 19th Century.

[23]Flint, *Recollections*, 261-262.

Crockett stuck his head through a small opening and yelled for help. His crew came to the rescue. "By a violent effort they jerked me through but I was in a pretty pickle when I got through. I had been sitting without any clothing over my shirt; this was torn off; and I was literally skin'd like a rabbit." All of the crewmen escaped on a raft, and another boat heading south picked them up. "This was the last of my boats and of my boating, for it went so badly with me that I hadn't much mind to try it any more."[24]

Given that rivermen faced tough challenges, they had to be tough men. Twain describes them as "rough and hardy men; rude, uneducated, brave, suffering terrific hardships with sailor-like stoicism; heavy drinkers, coarse frolickers . . . heavy fighters, reckless fellows, every one, elephantinely [sic] jolly, foul-witted, profane . . . yet, in the main, honest, trustworthy, faithful to promises and duty."[25] As Twain points out, it took "rough and hardy" men to shoulder the burdens of river travel. Keelboats hauled several tons of freight downriver using the current to help propel them, but going upriver proved to be a daunting experience with crews poling and pulling the boat forward. Men who stood out during the keelboat age, or at least those whose legends did, became folk heroes. Gould describes perhaps the most famous one. He calls Mike Fink a "leader of the men of his own class; and was famous for his herculean strength, his contempt of danger, his frolics, and his depredations. He was a coarse, vulgar, desperate man — yet possessed a degree of humor, hilarity, and openness that made him remarkable, and conciliated [sic] for him a sort of popularity, which caused him to be universally known, and still preserves his name in tradition. In his calling, as a master of a boat, he was faithful — a quality which seems to have belonged to most of his class; for it is a singular fact, that lawless and wild as these men were, the valuable cargoes of merchandise committed to their care, and secured by no other bond than their integrity, were always carried safely to the places of destination and the traveler, however weak, or however richly freighted, relied securely on their protection."[26] Such men generated many tall tales, short tales, and everything in between. An enduring story is author Thomas Banges Thorpe's *Big Bear of Arkansas,* which became a widely read classic. It appeared in a March 27, 1841, edition of the New York *Spirit of the Times.* In it the speaker describes to fellow steamboat passengers his impressions of Arkansas, "the creation state, the finishing-up country — a state where the sile [soil, one presumes] runs down to the centre of the 'arth, and government gives you a title to every inch of it. Then its airs — just breathe them, and they will make you snort like a horse. It's a state without a fault it is." "Excepting the mosquitoes," a knowledgeable listener observed.

---

[24]Stephen Brennan, editor, *An Autobiography of Davy Crockett* (New York: Skyhorse Publishing, 2011), 119-121. Crockett's ill-fated journey down the Mississippi River was one of many unfortunate trips, including one to the Alamo. Crockett's autobiography begins with his boyhood in Tennessee and includes service for Andrew Jackson during the War of 1812, politics, and a plethora of adventures and misadventures. Whether all these tales are entirely true or not, they make for lively stories.

[25]Twain, *Life*, 11.

[26]Gould, *73-74.*

Keelboat moving up the Mississippi River.
From a picture belonging to Mr. Pierre Choteau. Arkansas History Commission.

Flatboat headed down the Mississippi River.
From *Steamboat Times: A Pictorial History of the Mississippi Steamboating Era.*

Of the early rivercraft, according to Hunter flatboats "were slower to feel the effects of steamboat competition. They were not so much boats as great, clumsy boxes which any carpenter, handyman, or farmer could knock together out of rough lumber. Because flatboats were clumsy and had a substantial draft of water when loaded, their use on many streams was confined to brief periods in the spring and fall when they could be sent off on flood waters." The vessels often carried raw materials such as lumber, stone, and bricks, but sometimes farmers used them to transport produce for sale downriver. New Orleans became the most popular destination for flatboats.[27]

---

[27]Hunter, 54.

The Antebellums Arrive

The first recorded steamboat journey down the Mississippi River began in Pittsburgh, Pennsylvania. The boat belonged to Robert Fulton, Robert Livingston, and Nicholas Roosevelt, and they named it *New Orleans*. Piloted by Roosevelt, in 1811 the steamer set out for New Orleans, Louisiana with an eight-man crew, three servants, a cook, two friends, a pregnant wife, and a dog. All aboard had the misfortune of arriving at New Madrid, Missouri during a series of devastating earthquakes, but the boat and passengers survived. After stops along the way and taking on cotton in Natchez, Mississippi, the steamer docked at New Orleans during January 1812, completing an almost two-month journey. *New Orleans* then began commercial runs between New Orleans and Natchez. Fulton and his prominent partner, Robert Livingston of Louisiana Purchase fame, thought they had acquired exclusive rights to control steamboat traffic in Louisiana Purchase waterways, but they thought wrong. Many rivermen ignored their claim and ran their boats as they pleased. Unfortunately for the two businessmen, the restriction could not be enforced, and by 1819 more than 30 vessels of various sizes and designs worked in New Orleans-Pittsburgh trade.[28] Demand for steamboats became so great and their lifespan so brief, about two and one-half years, that shipyards collectively built approximately one boat per week between 1820 and 1860. Medium-sized vessels on average cost about $20,000. Large floating palaces ran $100,000 and up.

Destruction of many Mississippi riverboats in the early 1800s may be attributed indirectly to earthquakes. During 1811-1812 the so-called New Madrid earthquakes destroyed riverboats and changed river conduits dramatically. On December 15, 1811, the disaster began. With an epicenter near Arkansas's northeastern edge, people rushed outside their houses to save themselves from collapsing structures and found sulfuric vapors seeping through cracks in the ground. Tremors continued for days. Eliza Bryan, who lived near

Portrait of Robert Fulton, after a painting by Benjamin West.

New Madrid, Missouri, described the ensuing terror in this account repeated by author Norma Hayes Bagnall. "People could hear trees cracking and falling. Nearby, the Mississippi River roared without stop [claiming] riverbanks and forests of trees that tumbled into it." Bryan recalled the effect of quakes on the Mississippi and that "the river seemed to recede from its banks, and its waters gathered up like a mountain, leaving boats stranded

---

[28]Paul Schneider, *Old Man River. The Mississippi River in North American History* (New York: Henry Holt and Company, 2013), 247. Schneider traces the river from its paleo-Indian past to the British Petroleum oil spill. To tell his story the author draws upon diverse sources such as river tales and reports to describe a history that winds and loops like the river that runs through it.

A painting of *New Orleans*, credited with being the first steamboat to journey down the Mississippi River. Artist Gary R. Lucy.

on the sand."[29] At one point a wave about 20 feet high struck land, ripped boats from their moorings and carried them inward for about a quarter of a mile. Then the river returned violently to its banks. Quakes continued into 1812, and on February 7 of that year a severe eruption wreaked havoc on nearby boats on the Mississippi River. High waves crashed over the banks, then surged back, sinking vessels and killing their crews. Astonishingly, a violent dislocation reversed the mighty river's direction, and it ran backwards for a while, creating two waterfalls upriver from New Madrid. This hazard capsized more than 20 boats and killed their crewmen. As a result of the quakes, river channels relocated, several towns in three states disappeared, and some islands and lakes ceased to exist.

Despite the hurdles, increased steamboat traffic drew more people to Arkansas riverbanks to admire, board, ship, or possibly all three. They arrived by gumbo roads and pig paths to gaze in wonderment. Along with steamboats, another type of craft benefited from riverside crowds. Shantyboats began to swarm the rivers like Delta mosquitoes. Water-borne peddlers sold everything from dry goods, to trinkets, to produce. Salesmen with cure-all medicines found shantyboat life lucrative. Their only expense was for bottles. In the woods they found roots, barks, and herbs sufficient to give their product a bad taste and sickening appearance, proof positive of its efficacy. The only other ingredient necessary for their success was talk, and they were full of that.[30] Authors Herbert Quick and Edward Quick explain that "Gamblers and lottery operators

---

[29]Norma Hayes Bagnall, *On Shaky Ground: The New Madrid Earthquakes of 1811-1812* (Columbia: University of Missouri Press, 1996), 30-32. Estimates claim that more than 2,000 tremors struck the region, and three of them probably would have measured approximately 8.0 on the Richter Scale, a device not in existence at that time. The quakes were felt as far away as Canada and New Orleans, and in affected areas the earth remained in a state of constant motion for almost four months.

[30]Herbert Quick and Edward Quick, *Mississippi Steamboatin'. A History of Steamboating on the Mississippi and its Tributaries.* (New York: Henry Holt and Company, 1926), 118. The authors address all sections of the Lower Mississippi, including Ohio-Lower Mississippi trade routes. Their work starts with boats that preceded steamers and ends with an assessment of the steamboats' future. They cover the impact of major historic phases such as the Civil War and what they call "dry statistics" as well as colorful characters. Noteworthy is the fact that the authors completed this book in the 1920s and thus had no access to voluminous scholarship since then.

[also] drifted down the rivers, sometimes by themselves and sometimes with traveling saloons or with boats that carried two or three women from the vice districts of the northern cities, also small shows of a more or less shady sort." For atonement, or perhaps retribution, preachers on shantyboats held services in tents or in the open air, but not every clergyman "exhorting people to repentance was an honest to God divine. All too frequent were the impostors who shouted for temperance, took up collections for putting down the Demon Rum, and in their idle hours did their best to put down the demon direct from the mouth of the jug."[31]

Much of the Delta's growing river traffic plied the Arkansas, and Gould draws upon several press reports to describe this river's growing attraction. "What a country is this where there are rivers navigable for hundreds of miles which we are just beginning to hear of. Surely the Arkansas is just becoming known abroad. If one steamboat trip to within twelve miles of the Cherokee Missionary establishment at Dwight creates so much surprise among our Eastern brethren, how much more will they stare when they are told the steamboat *Robert Thompson* has actually made three passages this season to Fort Smith, about one hundred and twenty-five miles above Dwight, and upwards of five hundred miles from the Mississippi. Their astonishment will be considerably heightened undoubtedly when we have gone five hundred miles further [sic] without difficulty."[32]

In March 1820, *Comet* became the first steamboat to "venture up" to Arkansas Post, Arkansas, and two years late *Eagle* landed at Little Rock, Arkansas.

Gould quotes a reporter saying that the vision of boats steaming along Arkansas waterways "will be hailed with wonder and surprise by the aborigines of our country. And yet, however incredible it may appear to some, we have no doubt but that the time is not far distant when this sight will be familiar to them. It is but little more than two years since we witnessed the sight of the first steamboat at the town of Arkansas, and not yet four months since we announced the arrival of the first steamboat that ever ascended the Arkansas to this place. But that which was a novelty to many of our citizens a few months ago has become familiar to them. They have already witnessed four passages made a great distance into the interior of our country by steamboats, and in future will look for their return with the same regularity that they look for the return of the seasons."[33] Unfortunately for many Delta passengers, at that time most steamers on inland waterways "were not the large, well-equipped floating palaces that serviced the Mississippi," Dougan points out. Rather, they were small and often unpleasant. He describes one White River traveler's description of *Fox* as "a little, dirty, wheezing, asthmatic sternwheeler."[34] Passenger accommodations on early steamboats running Arkansas rivers tended to be spartan. Most of them had cramped quarters. The gentlemen's cabin offered upper and lower bunks with only curtains for privacy. The ladies' cabin provided small staterooms.[35] The influx of people may be traced in part to federal land policy begun in the 1820s whereby settlers could pay $1.25 per acre for 40 or 80 acres. A March 25, 1820 edition of the *Arkansas Gazette* reported that three boats arrived at Arkansas Post with families from Kentucky and

---

[31]Quick and Quick, 119-120.

[32]Gould, 281. Dwight refers to Dwight Mission established in 1820 near Russellville, Arkansas. It operated until 1829 as the first formal Protestant effort to educate and convert Native Americans.

[33]Gould, 281-282.

[34]Dougan, 118.

[35]Duane Huddleston, Sammie Cantrell Rose, and Pat Taylor Wood, *Steamboats and Ferries on the White River. A Heritage Revisited.* New Edition (Fayetteville: University of Arkansas Press, 1998), 23. The authors survey a wide variety of boats, from keelboats and flatboats to steamboats and ferries. Accompanied by a substantial collection of maps and illustrations, the narrative provides an extensive background on White River history.

Tennessee who planned to ascend the Arkansas River and settle in the vicinity of Fort Smith.

According to Gould, one steamer that frequented the Arkansas River was the aptly named *Buzzard*. He calls *Buzzard* a "worn-out, rickety old craft that had lost all favor with every insurance company from Pittsburgh to New Orleans." Despite the fact that inspectors pronounced the vessel unsafe, its "captain had the audacity to stick hand-bills on the corners and other conspicuous places announcing that the new, staunch, fast-sailing *Buzzard*, having splendid accommodations for passengers . . . would leave for Little Rock, Van Buren, and Fort Smith." The boat's captain proved to be a "wild, harum-scarum rough species of early rivermen." Other crewmen fit the same mold. "One day the *Buzzard* entered the lower end of a long reach. The engineer now set his engine and proceeded to the cabin, took a smile [sic] of whiskey and commenced to deal faro. The pilot lashed his wheel amidships, lit his pipe, and proceeded to the cabin to bet against the engineer and captain. The *Buzzard*, left to her own guidance, was going ahead finely on her own

account when she entered a chute, took a sudden plunge into the bank with uncommon velocity, crushed in her bow, and knocked a hole in her as large as a hogshead."

An Arkansas passenger knew right away that something was amiss. "'She's sinking,'" he shouted. "'Tomahawk me if she ain't sinking shure.'" Despite this crisis the steamboat's owner continued to play his fiddle. "'Three feet water in the hold,' shouted the captain, 'run the d—-d old *Buzzard* ashore, if you can.'" The owner heard these startling words, but continued to fiddle. "A passenger ran to him and bawled out, 'Did you know the boat was snagged?' 'I suspected something of the kind,' coolly answered the owner, as he laid his hand upon the violin. 'She'll be lost in five minutes,' shouted the passenger. 'She's been a losing concern for five years,' responded the owner, and went on playing his fiddle. The boat careened, [and] the next moment the cabin was half full of water. The *Buzzard* was a total loss. The owner swam ashore with his fiddle under his arm, his bow in his mouth."[36]

---

[36]Gould, 280-281.

Snags and Shreve

Though the Fulton partnership brought steam propulsion to the Mississippi River, it did not introduce a boat ideally suited for use there. That task fell to Henry Shreve. He knew that a deep hull, like the one on Fulton's craft, would not long survive the Mississippi's numerous impediments, such as sandbars and snags. So Shreve designed and built *Washington*. Because of its shallow hull, he located machinery on a lower deck. To increase space, Shreve put another deck atop that and a small pilothouse above. Though rather strange looking compared to the graceful boats designed by Fulton, the Shreve craft glided along Mississippi River channels and in and out of shallow water at plantation landings.[37] Author Diana Sherwood points out that Shreve additionally had the distinction of winning a legal and public relations contest that ended the Livingston and Fulton claim that "no steamboat built by others than themselves could be operated upon such rivers" in Louisiana Purchase territory. The two business partners "also decreed that all steamboat owners and operators must procure their licenses from them under penalty of a $1,000 fine and one year's imprisonment."[38] This monopoly, granted Fulton and Livingston by the Louisiana legislature, had important consequences for steamboat commerce on the Lower Mississippi, and author Robert Gudmestad lays out the twists and turns of the dispute.

The Fulton and Livingston operating entity, Ohio Steam-Boat Navigation Company, operated the steamer *New Orleans* and "hauled so many passengers and so much freight that it was rumored to have cleared $20,000 its first year." This led to the company launching *Vesuvius* and *Aetna* in 1814 and 1815. As one might expect, other boat operators wanted in on the action. Daniel French built *Enterprise* and hired Shreve to captain the boat. When Shreve steamed into New Orleans during May 1815 and prepared to depart, a deputy arrested him for violating the monopoly. Though the *Louisiana Courier* newspaper and Louisiana's

Washington, Shreve's shallow hull design. Public Library of Cincinnati and Hamilton County.

---

[37]Gandy and Gandy, 3.

[38]Diana Sherwood, "Clearing the Channel — the Snagboat in Arkansas." *Arkansas Historical Quarterly* 3:1 (Spring 1944), 55.

Painting of Henry Shreve clearing a log jam by Lloyd Hawthorne. Courtesy of R. W. Norton Art Gallery.

governor, William C. Claiborne, supported the Fulton company, many Louisiana residents did not, considering the arrangement an impediment to regional growth and interference by arrogant outsiders. As a result, other steamboats "chugged into New Orleans like so many pesky flies, and their steady presence showed . . . the impracticality of enforcing the monopoly."[39]

In New Orleans the Fulton company offered Shreve a 50 percent interest, but the captain declined and departed before he could be sued. Shreve returned in March 1817, and the city marshal arrested him amid an angry crowd of supporters. After a night in jail, Shreve left the city, and during the following April a judge dismissed the case over a jurisdictional issue. Gudmestad says that at that point "The Fulton-Livingston monopoly was dead. A tangled skein of troubles ultimately brought down the Ohio Steam-Boat Navigation Company."[40]

Shreve undertook many projects to improve transportation by boat, and clearing rivers of obstacles became one of them. To accomplish this he designed the snagboat. Granted a patent in 1824, Shreve's first two boats, *Heliopolis* and *Archimedes*, supported cranes that could remove large imbedded snags from a depth of 20 feet. Observers reported that one raised snag contained 1,600 cubic feet of lumber, the root alone weighing 60 tons. Each snagboat with a crew of 50 men removed an average of 20 pieces a day. To support this effort, Sherwood says that in 1830 the U. S. Congress appropriated $15,000 "for improving the navigation of the rivers in Arkansas, providing the Engineering Department, after due examination, is satisfied that during the portion of the ensuing year the men and machines now employed in removing obstructions from the Mississippi River can be more usefully employed in removing those from Arkansas's rivers."[41] One important consequence for the Delta involved clearing out areas at islands No. 62 and No. 63 at the confluence of the Arkansas and Mississippi rivers. There the current pushed snags and boats into a narrow channel, a deadly combination that claimed many vessels.

Despite improvements in Delta rivers during the decade, some Arkansas travelers found passage by boat extraordinarily unpleasant. Two missionaries, Cyrus Kingsbury and his brother-in-law, Alfred Finney, were especially critical of fellow passengers. After going by land to Walnut Hills near present-day Vicksburg, Mississippi, they boarded *Fayette* headed to the White River. Upon disembarking the two men "rejoiced at leaving the steamboat, where we had been so much pained by the filthy conversation of the wicked," according to Kingsbury's journal.[42]

---

[39]Robert Gudmestad, *Steamboats and the Rise of the Cotton Kingdom* (Baton Rouge: Louisiana State University Press, 1964), 15-16. Gudmestad explains the impact of steamboats and their cotton cargo on the southern economy, linking it to national and international markets. The consequences included forcing productivity increases out of enslaved workers, enriching the Cotton South's planter class, and creating a new river culture.

[40]Gudmestad, 15-17.

[41]Sherwood, 56-57.

[42]Cyrus Kingsbury, "Journal of the Mission Among the Cherokees of Arkansas," *Missionary Herald* 17 (May 30, 1820), 149.

A snagboat designed by Shreve. Louisiana Historical Association.

A Colonel Davis from Ohio offered them a place on his keelboat to Arkansas Post. They accepted, but still had problems with Delta culture, or the lack of it, observing that profanity, idleness, drinking, and gambling prevailed. The intrepid missionaries eventually reached Little Rock, where they anticipated a civilized citizenry, a questionable assumption.

During the late 1820s a growing number of steamboats worked Delta rivers, including *Alleghany, Florence, Spartan, Superior, Catawba, Velocipede,* and *Highland Laddie.*[43] According to the May 28, 1828, *Arkansas Gazette,* one entrepreneur brought regular service to the Arkansas River. The state's "most famous boatman, Captain Pennywit," scheduled roundtrips from Fort Gibson, Oklahoma through Little Rock to New Orleans about every 30 days when water levels permitted. Steamboat visits to rustic Delta locations generated excitement ashore. In 1828 an editor of the *Western Monthly Review* wrote that a steamer coming from New Orleans "brings to the remotest village of our streams, and the very doors of the cabins, a little Paris, a section of Broadway, or a slice of Philadelphia." He went on to itemize a boat's temptations, including "cards, and dice, and flirting, and love-making, and drinking."[44] In addition to providing occasions for sin, steamboats continued to haul people looking for a better life, not a debauched one. At one point more than 200 immigrants from Alabama, Tennessee, and Kentucky waited at the mouth of the White River for transportation up the Arkansas River. *Amulet*

[43]Walter Moffatt, "Transportation in Arkansas, 1819-1840," *Arkansas Historical Quarterly* 15: 3 (Autumn 1956), 195.

[44]Schneider, 251.

Steamboat Crew

In a September 1, 1940, edition of the *Arkansas Gazette*, John Q. Wolf described a typical steamboat crew, which consisted of the following, roughly in order of status.

A captain commanded the boat. He set departure schedules, controlled business matters, and schmoozed passengers.

The master served as executive officer and often owned the boat.

Pilots handled the wheel and controlled a steamer's course.

A clerk checked freight on and off the vessel to ensure it matched his manifest.

An assistant, called a mud clerk, accounted for freight on shore, often at soggy landings.

Engineers saw to the propulsion system, communicating with the pilot by using bells connecting the engine room with the pilothouse.

Firemen fed fuel into the furnace, probably the most arduous job on the vessel.

A mate managed deckhands in loading and unloading cargo.

Roustabouts hauled freight on and off the vessel. Most roustabouts and deckhands could not read, but could recognize numbers and letters. Therefore a shipment had a number or letter on it to identify where it would be off-loaded.

Deckhands handled freight while aboard the boat.

from Pittsburgh, Pennsylvania brought about 90 in March 1830 and *Waverly* approximately 190 during the same month.[45]

From the very first steamboat trip down the Mississippi River and many thereafter, New Orleans served as its southern anchor and an international port for shipping goods into and out of the United States. Cotton gathered from villages along the Mississippi River and its tributaries became a major export. Unfortunately, the city also developed a notorious slave market. In April 1828 Abraham Lincoln was hired by the owner of a cargo boat carrying produce from Ohio to New Orleans. Author Godfrey Charnwood reveals that during Lincoln's trip to the bustling port, he saw "negroes chained, maltreated, whipped and scourged." The future president and two friends "came in their rambles upon a slave auction where a fine mulatto girl was being pinched and prodded and trotted up and down the room like a horse to show how she moved." One of Lincoln's companions, John Hanks, recalled that when the future president observed the auction his heart bled. Lincoln told his friends, "'By God, boys, let's get away from this. If ever I get a chance to hit that thing, I'll hit it hard."[46] And hit it hard, he did.

Despite horrors below deck, cabin passengers passed many pleasant days as the 1830s progressed. Crews served meals in the main cabin, usually with china and silverware placed on linen cloths. Often a piano in the room provided entertainment. Occasionally passengers danced to the strains of a band or orchestra. Invariably there was a bar stocked with liquor. Bartenders leased space for about $50 per month from where they sold alcoholic beverages. One bartender on a vessel in New Orleans-Louisville trade claimed to have cleared $400 on a single trip. The amount of drinking on western steamboats was prodigious, Gudmestad reports,

---

[45]Mattie Brown, "River Transportation in Arkansas 1819-1890," *Arkansas Historical Quarterly* 1:4 (December 1942), 344.

[46]Godfrey Charnwood, *Abraham Lincoln. A Biography* (Lanham, MD: Madison Books, 1996), 18. Lincoln worked as a bow hand using the foremost oar and earned $8 per month from the day he started to the day he returned home.

quoting one traveler admitting that "Passengers are driven into the habit by mere listlessness."[47] A poker room located near the bar usually contained one or more professional gamblers, called slickers. If caught cheating, not a rare discovery, slickers were dumped on the next river island. Passing boats would not pick up a man standing alone on an island since their crews knew how and why he got there.

By 1833 several steamers were engaged in Arkansas River trade, mostly between Napoleon, Arkansas and Little Rock, but some to Fort Smith, Arkansas and beyond. As traffic increased, so did complaints about the river being an obstacle course. The need to clear rivers of snags and other dangerous obstacles led to the increased use of snagboats. In February 1834 a Little Rock newspaper announced that two of Shreve's snagboats, *Heliopolis* and *Archimedes*, had worked for the past three or four weeks removing snags, sawyers, and other obstructions from "our noble river." The newspaper cited sources claiming that rapid progress was being made clearing impediments. "Already they have removed most of the principal ones from the

mouth of the river to the Pine Bluffs, a distance of more than 140 miles, and when we last heard from them . . . they were several miles above the latter place progressing up stream." Such efforts led to a questionable conclusion by state authorities that the channel had been made "safe for navigation" and that the "heyday" of river transportation had begun.[48] However, reports prepared in 1833 described the Lower White River being choked with drifts, logs, and snags.

Danger to boats in the Delta came in the form of natural obstacles and those created by bandits. Author Jeannie Whayne says that in 1834 a posse went after outlaws operating out of a "rough-and-tumble camp" in the southern part of Mississippi County, Arkansas. Residents from Tennessee formed an expedition that set out to find and arrest thieves who raided riverboats and stole their cargo. Whayne explains that these outlaws "preyed on the ships and barges that navigated through the numerous snags and ever-shifting series of sandbars along the Plum Point reach, a treacherous seventeen-mile section of the Mississippi River." Fed up with these robberies, Tennesseans boarded

Typical Monthly Salaries of Officers on Western Steamboats, 1837-1880							
(In dollars)							
	1837	1843	1849	1855	1868	1874	1880
Captain	150	75	50-120	200	150-250	125	60-100
Clerk	50	50	40-100	150	125-150	100-125	45-100
Pilot	140	...	60-160	300	100-125	100-125	40-100
Engineer	125	40	50-100	150	100-125	100	50-60
Mate	...	30	30-60	150	100	75-100	30-60

Monthly salaries of officers on western steamboats, 1837-1880, varied significantly. Hunter points out that there were "three divisions in the society of the steamboat; the cabin passengers and officers, the deck passengers, and the rank and file of the crew."[49]

[47]Gudmestad, 40.

[48]Sherwood, 58-61.

[49] Hunter, 391, 445.

the steamboat *Kentuckian*, which carried them to Arkansas. "After slogging through nearly impenetrable terrain, they descended on the hideout, destroyed the camp, and "captured eight or ten of the suspects." The steamer *Tennessean* carried the prisoners across the Mississippi River. "Additional Arkansas expeditions seized more prisoners and stolen property." However, "Some of the outlaws eluded capture and disappeared further [sic] into the swamps, and the reputation of the Arkansas region for harboring such criminals persisted."[50]

As steamboat traffic increased, so did the size of vessels. Large steamers typically had a main deck on the bottom, where boilers were located, along with freight and deck passengers; next the boiler deck, which included passenger cabins and service areas (but no boilers); then the hurricane deck at the top. The texas was a cabin-like structure that sat on the hurricane deck (sometimes called the texas deck) and included quarters for the officers and crew. Atop this area was the pilothouse.

[50]Jeannie Whayne, *Delta Empire. Lee Wilson and the Transformation of Agriculture in the New South* (Baton Rouge: Louisiana State University Press, 2011), 9-10. Whayne tells an interesting story—-how the Lee Wilson family acquired thousands of acres of Delta farmland and created an empire. In doing so the author illuminates the people and forces that transformed plantations into modern agribusiness empires.

A Gothic Gleam

Delta scenery along rivers caught the fancy of several famous writers. Washington Irving watched it go by and wrote in his journals about the region's wilderness. Author Robert Morris mentions that during Irving's travels, including a stretch between Little Rock, Arkansas Post, and Montgomery Point, Arkansas, he "invested the frontier wilderness with a gothic gleam." While aboard the steamer *Little Rock*, Irving became impressed by what he saw along the way. He observed "groups of negroes in Sunday dress," a flock of pigeons perched on a sandbar, wooded banks with cottonwoods and willows, log cabins in settlements, cattle grazing along the shore in sunshine, bayous, and wild forests.[51] G. W. Featherstonhaugh, a British writer who rarely had much good to say about the region and its rivers, praised the White River. After an early 1830s journey he called it "one of the most important and beautiful rivers of North America."[52] The White River possessed the virtue that even during dry seasons it carried boats "mainly because of the numerous springs that gush forth in the Ozarks and drain into the White River,"[53] according to author Mabel West.

Many boat travelers found the springs valuable in other ways since they provided fresh drinking water. Passengers and crew often had difficulty drinking river water. It was so muddy that they had to store it in jars overnight before they could see through it.[54] River water also became dirty words for James Audubon, the famous artist who cruised rivers throughout the Lower Mississippi to locate scenes for his popular paintings. Audubon laments in journals a steamer's lack of basic amenities and refers to fellow passengers as the "dirtiest of the dirty." After he describes one vessel's bathing facilities one can understand why. "We had to dip the water for washing from the river in tin basins, soap ourselves all from the same cake, and wipe the one hundred and fifty [persons] with the same solitary one towel rolling over a pin." He calls fellow passengers on one steamer "Buckeyes, Wolverines, Suckers, Hoosiers, and gamblers, with drunkards of each and every denomination, their ladies and babies of the same nature."[55]

As critics raged, bands played, and flags waved, steamboat losses mounted. *Volant* and *Reindeer* both made White River runs during the 1830s and met an end common at the time. After departing New Orleans for the Arkansas River, *Reindeer* took on passengers at Vicksburg, Mississippi. Unfortunately, one of them had cholera, and it spread to other passengers and the crew. By the time *Reindeer* reached Montgomery Point, Arkansas, Captain Miller was sick. After a few hours he succumbed to the disease. The boat proceeded to Little Rock, and by then six more passengers and crew members were dead, including the pilot and engineer. Another passenger died at the city. After being "scrubbed" the vessel continued upriver

---

[51]Robert L. Morris, "Three Arkansas Travelers." *Arkansas Historical Quarterly* 14: 3 (Autumn 1945), 222-223.

[52]G. W. Featherstonhaugh, *Excursion Through the Slave States* (New York: Harper and Brothers, 1844), 89. A geologist, Featherstonhaugh was commissioned to undertake a survey of Arkansas Territory and spent 1834-1835 travelling through the southern slave states to reach his destination. He was shocked by the slave system of the South and wrote about it candidly, though his manuscript remained unpublished until after his return to England. His work is a mixture of scientific and sociological detail about the region.

[53]Mabel West, "Jacksonport, Arkansas: Its Rise and Decline," *Arkansas Historical Quarterly* 9: 4 (Winter 1950), 234-235.

[54]Quick and Quick, 111.

[55]Maria Audubon and Elliott Coues, editors, *Audubon and His Journals*, 2 volumes (New York: Scribner's Sons, 1897), 1, 451. Audubon studied birds over many decades in the southern wilderness. The artist's quest led him down backroads and through bayous and resulted in brilliant paintings and publication of his artistic masterpiece, *The Birds of America*.

to Fort Smith, Arkansas. One more crew member died on the way. The vessel's luck remained bad. In June 1833, owners sold *Volant* and *Reindeer*. While being dismantled at New Albany, Indiana, fire struck *Volant* and spread to *Reindeer*. Flames consumed both boats.[56]

Other vessels had more success in White River trade. *William Purson* ran to Jaque's Creek near Jacksonport, Arkansas in 1833. Others working the White River included *Sam Ham, Julia Dean,* and *Osage*, which came up from Memphis and Little Rock about three times a week. *Chickasaw, Lady Boone,* and *Steubenville* went as far as the Upper White, according to the September 11, 1833, *Arkansas Gazette. Mount Vernon* serviced Batesville, Arkansas. Food and supplies hauled by these vessels and others could be critical to many Arkansans living along rivers. According to news accounts, availability of groceries from river traffic dropped prices by more than 50 percent in Batesville. The price of coffee went from 50 cents a pound to 20 cents. Sugar dropped from 25 cents a pound to ten cents. Arkansas riverboat traffic became so heavy that in 1833 the *Arkansas Gazette* commenced printing a Little Rock register listing vessels, dates of arrival, cargoes, and names of passengers.

Though convenience and reliability of steamboats continued to grow, improvements sometimes did not compensate for the unpleasantness of some fellow travelers. Featherstonhaugh's opinions about Arkansans he met during riverboat travel on the White River are unabashedly negative. "I had been told at the post of Arkansas that ten passengers were waiting to come on board, and that several of them were notorious swindlers and gamblers, who, whilst in Arkansas, lived by the most desperate cheating and bullying, and who skulked about alternately betwixt Little Rock,

Natchez, and New Orleans in search of any plunder that violent and base means could bring into their hands. Very soon after I had retired to the steamer at sun-set, the whole clique came on board, and the effect produced on us was something like that which would be made upon passengers in a peaceful vessel forcibly boarded by pirates of the most desperate character." These bullies took over the cabin, and "red-hot with whiskey they crowded round the stove and excluded all the old passengers. Armed with pistols and knives, expressly made for cutting and stabbing . . . they commenced spitting, smoking, cursing and swearing, drawn from the most remorseless pages of blasphemy."[57]

Other despicable passengers used riverboats to transport enslaved men and women to market. A letter to the editor published in a New York *Emancipator* 1834 edition provided a lamentable description of their horrific treatment. "They are stowed away on the decks of steamboats . . . males and females, old and young, usually chained, subject to the jeers and taunts of passengers and navigators, and often, by bribes, or threats, or the lash, made subject to abominations not to be named. On the same deck you may see horses and human beings, tenants of the same apartments, and going to supply the same market. The dumb beasts, being less manageable, are allowed the first place, while the humans are forced into spare corners and vacant places." [58]

Despite horrific treatment and deplorable conditions for some travelers, others fared better and made smaller Delta rivers popular thoroughfares. By the mid-1830s regular boat service stretched up the St. Francis River. *Gladiator* set a record by steaming up that river to the town of St. Francis, Arkansas from New Orleans in only six days, reported a February 16, 1836, *Arkansas Gazette*. Author Effie Allison Wall claims that

---

[56]Huddleston, 19.

[57]Featherstonhaugh, 2, 237-245.

[58]Schneider, 258-259.

the first steamboat on the St. Francis River was *Wheeling*, an old sternwheeler.[59] Although Captain Thomas R. Bowman did not command the first steamer on the St. Francis River, he captained many others. Bowman became a prominent boatman on the river with a sternwheeler named *Plow Boy*. He transported game, hides, and fur for Memphis trade that he bought from trappers. Success enabled Bowman to construct a larger steamboat, *St. Francis No. 1*, which the captain operated for several years until he built *St. Francis No. 2*. Unfortunately, Confederates commandeered this steamer during the war, and it burned at Little Rock. After the conflict, Bowman commanded *Molly Hambleton* and constructed *St. Francis No. 3*. This expensive vessel cost him dearly, and a business downturn forced Bowman to sell. Financial distress sank the captain's steamboat career.

In addition to more freight hauled on small Delta rivers, steamboats continued to transport more people. A May 6, 1836, edition of the *Arkansas Advocate* reported the following. "The *Mount Pleasant* arrived Monday morning last with full freight and crowded with passengers, emigrants to this place [Little Rock] and other parts of the territory, among whom were several families." The May 6 edition announced that the "steamboat *Arkansas* arrived here today from New Orleans with 100 cabin, 95 deck passengers, and 125 tons of freight." Many newcomers with financial means settled on the flat, black soil along the Mississippi River, where land and weather made bountiful cotton crops and spawned large plantations. Featherstonhaugh calls central and northern Arkansas "rough and uncouth," but adds that "life in the cotton growing section was less rigorous." The Englishman admits being "visibly impressed with the large cargo of baled cotton," that was loaded from landings along the Arkansas River.[60]

Prior to 1836, individuals typically owned steamboats, but soon some company boats appeared throughout the region. They were not owned at first by stock companies in the modern sense of the term. Rather, owners pooled their vessels to achieve pricing and market share advantages. This arrangement changed after regular stock companies appeared during the 1850s. The popularity of this business model stemmed in large part from the need to spread risk of financial losses if a vessel went under, an all-too-common occurrence. One of the worst steamboat disasters during the 1830s involved the steamer *Moselle*. Its boilers exploded on the Ohio River during April 1838 killing many passengers and crewmen. An investigation of the disaster reverberated down the Mississippi River and into the Delta. Dr. John Locke, a chemistry professor at the Medical College of Ohio, led an inquiry. After outlining his technical findings in a report, Locke spoke unsparingly of a culture that tolerated if not promoted the underlying, systemic causes of so much destruction and death. In his report, the doctor stated that boiler explosions "have their foundation in the present mammoth evil of our country, in inordinate love of gain. We are not satisfied with getting rich, but we must get rich in a day. We are not satisfied with traveling at a speed of ten miles an hour, but we must fly. Such is the effect of competition, that everything must be done cheap; boiler iron must be cheap, traveling must be done cheap, freight must be cheap, yet everything must be speedy. A steamboat must establish a reputation of a few minutes swifter in a hundred miles than others before she can make fortunes fast enough to satisfy the owners. Also this seems to be demanded by the blind tyranny of custom, and the common consent of the community."[61]

---

[59]Effie Allison Wall, "Early Boating on St. Francis and Interesting Reminiscences as Told By Mrs. Margaret Clark," *Arkansas Historical Quarterly* 7: 3 (Autumn 1948), 227.

[60]Jack B. Scroggs, "Arkansas Statehood: A Study in State and National Political Schism," *Arkansas Historical Quarterly* 20: 3 (Autumn 1961), 229.

[61]Way, *Horns*, 22.

1838 explosion of the *Mozelle*. Ohio History Connection

Another gruesome accident occurred when *General Brown* exploded at Helena, Arkansas. A December 5, 1838, *Arkansas Gazette* story explained that the vessel's rapidly fired-up boilers "built up too much steam." When the boat shoved off, a boiler exploded with enormous force, and only two of the steamer's officers survived. The blast launched a clerk into the air, and he fell through the roof of a wharfboat. About 45 people died, either drowned or scalded to death. During this decade, the life of steamboats averaged less than three years, and nearly every edition of the *Arkansas Gazette* carried a story of one or more boating mishaps. Sometimes one edition contained several notices of catastrophes. The ongoing carnage brought outrage from the newspaper's editor, who declared that practically every mail delivery brought news of disasters and that in many cases the causes were due to "inefficiency and carelessness." The journalist stressed the need for "more careful steamboat inspection, more sobriety among the crews, better firefighting equipment, and more efficient night watchmen."[62] Despite complaints,

warnings, and recommendations, river travel remained dangerous.

Probably the greatest steamboat tragedy during the decade involved *Monmouth*. Author James T. Lloyd has some strong things to say regarding the cause of that disaster. Lloyd says that "we might call the awful catastrophe about to be particularized [sic] a massacre, a wholesale assassination, or anything but an accident. In some instances, and this is one of them, a reckless disregard of human life, when it leads to a fatal result, can claim no distinction, on any correct principle of law or justice, from wilful and premeditated murder." Near the end of 1837 *Monmouth* departed New Orleans for the Arkansas River "having been chartered by the U. S. government to convey about seven hundred Indians to the region which had been selected for their future abode." *Monmouth* reached Prophet Island, Arkansas bend at night and met *Tremont* being towed downriver by the steamer *Warren*. "Owing partly to the dense obscurity of the night, but much more to the mismanagement of the officers

---

[62]Walter Moffatt, "Transportation in Arkansas, 1819-1840," *Arkansas Historical Quarterly* 15:3 (Autumn 1956), 198-199.

Monmouth. From 1998 watercolor by Paul Bender.

of *Monmouth*, a collision took place between that vessel and *Tremont*, and such was the violence of the concussion, that *Monmouth* immediately sunk. "The unhappy red men, with their wives and children, were precipitated [sic] into the water; and such was the confusion which prevailed at the time, such was the number of the drowning people [that] more than half of the unfortunate Creeks perished. The captains and crews of the steamers *Warren* and *Yazoo*, by dint of great exertion, succeeded in saving about three hundred of the poor Indians, the remaining four hundred had become accusing spirits before the tribunal of a just God where they, whose criminal negligence was the cause of this calamity, will certainly be held accountable." Lloyd makes clear the primary cause of this collision. "The mishap, as we have hinted before, may be ascribed to the mismanagement of the officers of *Monmouth*. This boat was running in a part of the river where, by the usages of the river and the rules adopted for the better regulation of steam navigation on the Mississippi, she had no right to go

and where, of course, the descending vessels did not expect to meet with any boat coming in an opposite direction.

"It is not without some feeling of indignation that we mention the circumstances that the drowning of four hundred Indians, the largest number of human beings ever sacrificed in a steamboat disaster, attracted but little attention (comparatively speaking) in any part of the country. Even the journalists and news-collectors of that region, on the waters of which this horrible affair took place, appear to have regarded the event as of too little importance to deserve any particular detail; and accordingly the best accounts we have of the matter merely state the outlines of the story, with scarcely a word of commiseration for the sufferers, or a single expression of rebuke for the heartless villains who wantonly exposed the lives of so many artless and confiding people to imminent peril, or almost certain destruction."[63]

---

[63]James T. Lloyd, *Lloyd's Steamboat Directory and Disasters on the Western Waters* (Cincinnati: James T. Lloyd & Co., 1856), 126-127. This was the first general reference available on the subject of American riverboats. Lloyd's book includes full accounts of steamboat disasters from the first application of steam to publication of his book.

Despite such disasters, steamboats continued to remove Native Americans from and through the Delta. Steamers not only brought in settlers who coveted the fertile land, boats hauled away natives that previously lived there. President Andrew Jackson, who strongly favored confiscation of Native American land, used the 1830 Indian Removal Act to justify this injustice. Gudmestad believes that approximately 35,700 Native Americans of the 60,600 removed "traveled all or part of the way to Oklahoma in riverboats," many of them through the Delta.[64] Of the roughly 14,000 Choctaws taken from their northern Mississippi homes during 1831-1833, almost 11,000 went by steamboat. Authorities dumped approximately 3,000 of them at Arkansas Post, Arkansas and nearly 3,500 at Rock Roe, Arkansas, now the location of Clarendon, to await steamers for transportation to Oklahoma. About 4,200 Seminoles traveled through Little Rock on their way to Indian Territory. Many of the displaced people waiting in the Delta languished for months without proper provisions or protection from the weather.

Conditions on riverboats were not much better, but authorities preferred that mode of transportation. Army escorts could turn steamers into prisons, reducing escapes that occurred more frequently during land travel. Boat confinement also allowed authorities to eliminate or limit access to alcoholic beverages, which could make prisoners unruly. The fact that often these steamers were overloaded with people and understocked with necessities did not seem to bother most officials or private contractors who provided transportation. An undated New Orleans *True American* article proposed that "avaricious disposition to increase profits" led to deplorable treatment of Native Americans being held "in a state unfit for human beings." Gudmestad relates the experience of Doctor C. Lillybridge, a New York physician who "shivered alongside a group of Cherokees as they traveled to Little Rock. Sickness ravaged the group. Many died, their bodies wrapped in blankets and thrown overboard."[65] Such miserable conditions should have shocked even the most callous Americans and perhaps led to intervention, but few people knew about these atrocities. Officials and gullible journalists helped keep the injustice out of sight. An *Arkansas Gazette* on December 2, 1831, reported that Choctaw Indians expressed "much satisfaction with the arrangements which have been made for their comfort." Gudmestad calls the treatment of Native Americans a wretched affair from beginning to end, and so it was.

Boat owners also imposed shameful conditions on deck passengers, who paid little for the ride and got little in return. They were crammed into tight spaces without necessary facilities. In summer they sweltered; in winter they froze. These unfortunate people sometimes had to share bunks with vermin. One traveler found a rag on his bunk with moving "little white animals. The mere sight of them gave me the sensation of crawling and biting."[66] If no bunks were available, folks often slept on an excrement-covered deck. They had to bring food aboard, bribe the crew for scraps, or go hungry. "As a rule, bologna sausages, dried herring, water crackers, cheese, and a bottle of whiskey constituted the bill of fare."[67] This treatment spread diseases rapidly among them. Gudmestad quotes a U. S. Treasury secretary report that claimed "the main deck generally presents a scene of filth and wretchedness that baffles all description."[68] According to Hunter, "The chief and almost only virtue of deck passage was its cheapness. In 1830, deck passage from New Orleans to Louisville cost between $8 to $10 dollars. Steamboat owners made little distinction between these passengers and freight."[69]

---

[64]Gudmestad, 82.

[65]Gudmestad, 92.

[66]Hunter, 423.

[67]Hunter, 425.

[68]Gudmestad, 58.

[69]Hunter, 425.

Boats Built, Destroyed, or Noteworthy: 1830s

Bob Handy: a 47-ton steamer that ran the White River during the 1830s.

Harp: contracted to transport provisions to Native Americans along the Arkansas River. The boat snagged and sank on that river during 1838. (Huddleston, 21.)

Laurel: made two trips up the White River to Batesville, Arkansas during February 1831. The small vessel drew only two feet when fully loaded and hauled freight on low water when larger steamers could not. (Krivor, Final Report, Vol. 1, 90.)

Lioness: Probably during the early 1830s this steamer came to an ignominious end. Several kegs of gunpowder were stored in the cargo hold. When two crew members, apparently nitwits, went into the hold to rearrange freight they lit candles and blew up the boat, reducing it to "splinters." (Gudmestad, 114.)

Mount Vernon: A May 1838 edition of the Batesville *News* announced that this packet would operate from the mouths of the Arkansas and White rivers up to Batesville, Arkansas.

Neosho: snagged and sank during February 1837 approximately one mile above Judge Lucas' plantation on the Arkansas River near Arkansas Post; one person died. (Huddleston, 21.)

Ottawa: Little Rock merchants Ficklin and Rapley bought this steamer for their shipping in order to control costs and schedules, according to the May 29, 1834, *Arkansas Gazette.* Unfortunately, it sank in May 1834 below Little Rock on the Arkansas.

Rob Roy: collapsed a flue on the Mississippi River about four miles above Columbia, Arkansas in May 1836; eight persons died and 14 were badly scalded. (Lloyd, 292.)

Steubenville: According to the October 8, 1840, Batesville *News,* in January 1839 the vessel commenced running Arkansas and White rivers, but became disabled and abandoned in 1840.

Tecumseh: ran into a snag and went down in August 1838 about 18 miles below Little Rock. (Huddleston, 21.)

Washington: While bound from New Orleans to St. Louis a boiler burst in November 1839 near the mouth of the Arkansas River. "The boilers, engines, and upper works were entirely demolished. In fact, there never was a more terrific explosion. The *Washington* had just started from a wood-yard and was under full headway when the explosion took place. The boat was completely riddled with pieces of iron flying through the cabin. The dead were buried at the mouth of the Arkansas River." (Lloyd, 145.)

William Hurlbert: In 1838 this vessel became the first packet known to run as a regular mail carrier on a portion of the White River. It operated from Memphis to the mouth of the White River, then upriver to Rock Roe, a site opposite Clarendon, Arkansas. From that point on, stagecoaches carried the mail to Little Rock and other locations. (Huddleston, 22-23.)

William Parsons: Thomas Todd Tunstall, who would help establish Jacksonport, Arkansas in 1839, bought this steamer at New Orleans during 1833. In the spring of 1835 it struck a snag about 40 miles above Arkansas Post on the Arkansas River. The object knocked a hole in the hull, so Tunstall ran the steamer onto a sandbar. Unfortunately a drop of several feet in the river damaged the boat beyond repair. (Huddleston, 20-21.)

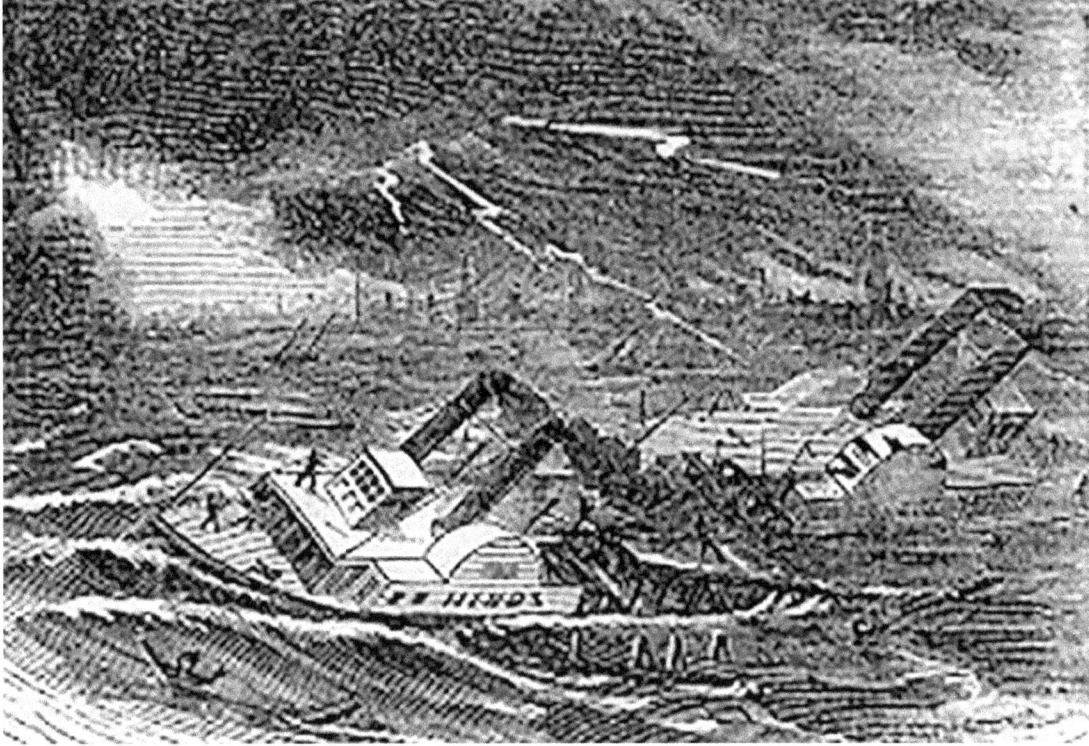

Hinds being torn apart by a storm in Natchez, Mississippi. *Lloyds Steamboat Directory*.

Upwards of 200 lives were lost when *Stonewall* burned at Neely's Landing, Missouri enroute to New Orleans. The fire broke out after a deck passenger knocked over a candle being used to light an evening card game. *Frank Leslie's Illustrated Newspaper*, Nov. 13, 1869. Library of Congress.

Infernal Contrivances

The average life of steamers due to natural causes and man-made was less than three years. Riverboat destruction came about from a variety of sources, but especially terrifying were storms and tornadoes, all too common along the Lower Mississippi. Captain J. H. Freligh of the steamer *Prairie* recounted his experiences with one in an article published by the St. Louis *Daily Commercial Bulletin* on June 9, 1840. Though it occurred at Natchez, Mississippi, this storm's effects typified what happened in these situations. Freligh recalled that a dark sky, rolling thunder, and lightning preceded the worst of the storm. "Suddenly the appearance of the sky changed, and showed by various signs the approach of a mighty wind. All were on the alert—-additional lines were ordered to be got out to shore—-the engineer ordered to be ready—-the pilot summoned to the wheel, and every precaution taken to have the boat secure against the storm. With one of the hands I ran to the roof to pay [sic] out a hawser to the forecastle. We had got the end out, and it was laid hold of by the men below, the hand and myself paying it out on the roof, when the storm burst upon us.

"With impulse of self-preservation, I sprang to the gangway leading to the boiler deck — plunged down it — and threw myself flat on my face on the boiler deck — grasped the edge of it to keep myself from being hurled away — looked up and saw the place I had just been standing on, and the entire works of the boat, swept away. The hand that was with me on the roof was precipitated [sic] to the forecastle uninjured. I lay, utterly incapable of motion from the violence of the wind about ten minutes."

When the wind abated, the captain ascertained that "the boat had parted all other moorings, and was turned stern up stream — her bow still being to the shore. She was again made fast, the waves pitching dreadfully. I looked around me — all was horror, desolation, ruin. Houses were laid level with the earth — the shore was entirely covered with the wreck of buildings, boats and goods. Two steamboats were sunk — fifty or more flatboats engulfed in the raging waters with their contents and their crews. My own boat lay a dismantled and useless wreck, floating a shapeless hulk on the boiling and maddened waters."

One Arkansan did not need a tornado to convince him of riverboat dangers. An unidentified newspaper reported in 1843 that a fed-up Arkansas traveler wearing a coonskin hat walked off a steamboat tied up for repairs. Though other passengers urged him to return to the vessel, he disagreed. "No, this is the last time I ever mean to put my foot in one of those eternal [probably infernal] contrivances. I have been five times run high and dry on a sand bank, four times snagged, three times sawyered, and twice blown up sky-high. I calculate I have given these creatures a pretty fair trial, and darn my breeches if I ever trust my carcass in one again. Take care of my plunder. I will call for it at St Louis." This steamboat customer may not have been impressed by a December 1844 Arkansas General Assembly declaration calling the White River navigable for boats from its confluence with the Mississippi River to the mouth of Swan Creek near Forsyth, Missouri.[70]

---

[70]Huddleston, 27.

Princess taking on wood to fire its boilers. Currier and Ives.

Stopping for Wood

When a vessel's fuel supply dwindled, its pilot pulled into the first woodyard he reached, generally located four to five miles apart along rivers. Sometimes fuel appeared at a plantation landing, cut and stacked there, but often fuel came from isolated sites. According to Huddleston, those who owned wood did not have to be present. If his wood was picked up, the owner went to a convenient landing when the boat was due and presented his bill. Theft of cordwood stacked along Delta rivers was "almost unknown." If a steamer became dangerously low of fuel and could find no woodyard, the boat landed near a farm, and crewmen removed boards from the farmer's rail fence. This wood fetched a stiff price. If still no luck, crews disembarked and chopped down trees.[71]

In about 1850, steamers consumed up to 30 cords a day at a cost of two to three dollars per cord. Boats continually sought to stay ahead of other vessels and be first to reach woodyards. Author Joseph Field describes one such spectacle. After a boat reached the bank, tied up, and dropped gangways, crewmen and deck passengers, who were required to help load wood to pay for their passage, dashed ashore. "Now ensues a scene that tasks description!" A fire ashore fueled by piles of wood "crimsons the tangled forest!" Using light from the fire to perform their task, "Black and white, many of them stripped to their waist, attack the lengthened pile . . . amid laugh, shout, curse, and the scarcely intermitting scream of the iron chimneys." When the mate and captain spotted a rival steamer they dashed ashore to "rush" the matter. "The bell is struck for starting, [and] amid a chaos of timber, a whirl of steam, and a crash of machinery, once more she is under weigh [sic]."[72]

---

[71]Huddleston, 27.

[72]Joseph M. Field, "Stopping for Wood," *Before Mark Twain: A Sampler of Old, Old Times on the Mississippi*, John Francis McDermott, editor (Carbondale: Southern Illinois University Press, 1968), 262. This book contains a collection of firsthand stories and observations from early travelers on the river.

Boats Built, Destroyed, or Noteworthy: 1840s

Arkansas No. 6: Ann James expressed her dissatisfaction with boat travel on a trip from New York City to Arkansas in January 1847. Author Deane G. Carter tells why James's journey up the Arkansas River became so disagreeable. The steamboat on which she booked passage was chartered to transport Native Americans, and "the Indians refused to travel after sunset." This required the boat to tie up every night. A major delay occurred when the steamer lodged on a sandbar. *Arkansas No. 6* picked up the passengers, but James' difficulties continued. She called the small vessel "a perfect toy boat; its tiny stove with thin tin stovepipe scarcely gave out any heat, and as it was very, very cold, we suffered. There were no state rooms, only thin, dark curtains to hide one bed from another. Its little tin window-frames allowed the snow to drift in onto the beds during the night." Eventually this steamer delivered her safely to Van Buren, Arkansas where James departed for Fayetteville, Arkansas.[73]

Batesville: sternwheel packet (1844) ran primarily on Arkansas and White rivers until dismantled in 1849. (Way, 38-39.) This is one of several boats named *Batesville* that operated in the region.

Bayou Boeuf: sternwheel packet (1847) sank at Clear Lake, Arkansas in March 1848. (Way, 39.)

Belle Zane: sternwheel packet (1844) snagged on the Mississippi River about 12 miles below the White River while headed for New Orleans in December 1845. It turned bottom-up, causing the deaths of 40 persons. (Way, 46.)

Delta: sternwheel packet with a hull built at Batesville, Arkansas and finished out in New Orleans during 1846. (Way, 123.)

Emily: sidewheel packet (1849) ran into a snag and was destroyed on the White River in August 1852. (Way, 148.)

General Lane: sidewheel packet (1848) struck a snag and went down at the mouth of the St. Francis River in December 1851. (Way, 181.)

General Shields: sternwheel packet (1849) hit a snag and sank in the Arkansas River during 1851. (Way, 183.)

Governor Bent: transported to Batesville, Arkansas in December 1847 the body of Captain Andrew R. Porter, a "hero" who died in the war with Mexico. During spring 1849 the vessel carried Captain Joseph Anthony to Pocahontas, Arkansas where he died of cholera after arriving. Two Arkansas passengers succumbed on the boat, and another died at Jacksonport, Arkansas after going ashore. (Huddleston, 28.) The steamer's run of bad luck continued in May of that year when its boilers exploded on the Mississippi River; one fireman died. Prior to the explosion, as many of the crew relaxed on the boiler deck, their attention was attracted to a rat, which they pursued, except for the one man who was killed. Had the rat not appeared at that moment, the crew would have been decimated. (Lloyd, 288.)

Gulnare: struck by *Westwood* in September 1844 about 20 miles above Helena, Arkansas. *Gulnare* sank within three minutes. "Passengers and crew escaped, with the exception of two Germans and a United States soldier, who were deck passengers. These three persons were drowned. The soldier was much intoxicated. One of the Germans lost his life while attempting to save his baggage." (Lloyd, 259.)

---

[73]Deane G. Carter, "A Place in History for Ann James," *Arkansas Historical Quarterly* 18:4 (Winter 1969), 315.

Hector: burned on the Mississippi River near Island No. 74 about two miles above Napoleon, Arkansas in November 1842; one passenger and a crewman perished. (Lloyd, 292.)

Julia: sidewheel packet (1848) snagged and lost in the Arkansas River during December 1860. (Way, 260.)

Nick of the Woods: a mail boat making regular trips on the White River during the 1840s, but sank during 1844 at an unknown location. *Rolla* temporarily took over the run until replaced by *Burkville.*

Persian: flues collapsed in November 1840 on the Mississippi River roughly three miles below Napoleon, Arkansas. According to a rumor, the captain was asleep at the time and the pilot was intoxicated when the steamer stopped to take on wood. The explosion killed six persons instantly; 17 died the following day, and 15 or 16 others were mortally wounded. The captain escaped without injury. (Lloyd, 169.)

Philip Pennywitt: sidewheel packet (1849) snagged and lost at Van Buren, Arkansas in May 1851. (Way, 370.)

Revenue: sidewheel packet (1844) made tramp trades to the Arkansas River and burned near Peoria, Illinois in May 1847. (Way, 392.)

Ringgold: sidewheel packet (1846) alerted Zachary Taylor at his Spithead Point plantation that he had been nominated for the U. S. presidency. The vessel snagged and sank in the Arkansas River during February 1848. (Way, 394.)

Sallie Anderson: sidewheel packet (1846) burned at Little Rock in September 1849. (Way, 415.)

Sultana: not the version that exploded at the end of the Civil War. This model collided with the steamer *Gray Eagle* at Island No. 35 on the Mississippi River in June 1848. Two *Gray Eagle* crewmen died, and five were wounded. (Lloyd, 284.)

Thomas Jefferson: went down during 1849 several miles above the mouth of the St. Francis River. (Stewart-Abernathy, 8.)

Victoria: Once owned by Cherokee Chief John Ross, he used the steamer to transport Native Americans. In 1840 the boat ran between Batesville, Arkansas and New Orleans. (Huddleston, 24.)

Wabash Valley: Apparently the steamer *Bulletin* struck this vessel, if correctly reported in the April 27, 1846, *Arkansas Gazette.* The reporter claimed that "I never heard of so wanton a sporting with human life before. The pilot of the *Bulletin* should be gibbetted." A witness indicated that *Bulletin* never stopped "though the *Valley's* distress bell was rang immediately. After the collision, but for the parting of the cabin from the hull, many would have drowned."

William Armstrong: sternwheel packet (1846) snagged and lost at Little Rock in November 1849. (Way, 487.)

Two Mighty Men

Fires became an increasing cause of riverboat destruction during the 1850s. Contributing factors probably included increased cotton shipping. Author Charles Bolton explains that during 1840, Arkansas yielded 15 bales of cotton for each 100 persons in the state. Late in the 1850s the state produced 84 bales for each 100. Great Britain's mills consumed the South's supply of the fiber and sought more. Increased production was related to more enslaved persons in the state and their concentration in the hands of cotton producers. Author Charles Bolten says that unfortunately, "Arkansas became more and more to be characterized by cotton and slavery."[74] Many southern states could make that claim. Until the Civil War, cotton and slavery expanded "in lockstep, as Great Britain and the United States had become the twin hubs of the merging empire of cotton," according to author Sven Beckert.[75] Cotton production wore out enslaved workers and the soil as well. A Georgia planter complained that "We appear to have one rule . . . to make as much cotton as we can, and wear out as much land as we can."[76] When cotton yields plunged in the Southeast, planters headed west to states such as Arkansas.

The big river and many smaller ones provided convenient access to plantation landings where bales waited. Surging cotton freight made New Orleans a key port for shipping abroad. As a result of expansion westward and many regional avenues to transport the crop, in 1860 Arkansas, Louisiana, Oklahoma, and Texas altogether produced 1,576,594 bales.[77] As a result of climbing farm production and other financial developments, commercial centers grew up along Delta waterways. Little Rock and other Arkansas towns became business hubs, including Batesville, Jacksonport, Newport, and Pine Bluff. Located on the Mississippi River, Napoleon and Helena prospered, too. Villages and towns along rivers with boat access decreased the need for other forms of transportation. This was a good thing since, as author Thomas A. DeBlack points out, travel by land was a "slow, arduous, and often dangerous endeavor. The national railroad-building boom of the 1840s and 1850s barely touched Arkansas," and unfortunately, "stagecoach travel over the state's primitive roads was a bone-jarring test of endurance."[78] Apparently this was a regional problem. Gudmestad repeats a British traveler's complaint that "no one can imagine what a bad road is until he has travelled in the Western States of America."[79]

Even though railroad cars and stagecoaches continued to be inconvenient options for many travelers, at least they did not blow up in spectacular fashion. Roughly 25 steamboats exploded every year between 1848 and 1852 in the Mississippi basin, killing more than 1,100 passengers and

---

[74]Charles Bolton, *Arkansas, 1800-1860. Remote and Restless.* (Fayetteville: University of Arkansas Press, 1998), 62. Bolton describes migration into Arkansas, mostly from other southern states, and chronicles growth of the agricultural economy.

[75]Sven Beckert, *Empire of Cotton. A Global History* (New York: Alfred A. Knopf, 2014), 103. Beckert examines cotton's place in the world economy and connects it to an evolving global capitalism. The fiber helped advance an industry, slave labor, Cotton South income, and steamboat shipping. It brought first riches then ruin to the American South and turmoil between factory owners and workers throughout the world. Beckert follows the many threads that created the empire and held it together.

[76]Beckert, 103.

[77]Beckert, 352.

[78]Thomas A. DeBlack, *With Fire and Sword, Arkansas, 1861-1874* (Fayetteville: University of Arkansas Press, 2003), 4. This is volume four in the Histories of Arkansas series. In it DeBlack discusses how the Civil War rendered a once prosperous state into one riven with political discord and suffering from economic ruin. In his story the author provides a view of the famous, infamous, and ordinary.

[79]Gudmestad, 10.

crewmen. Authorities supposedly governed steamer safety in the form of hull and boiler inspectors, but Way explains how this process actually worked. "Let those two dignitaries set foot on the forward gangway of any steamboat and the whole atmosphere was charged with adrenaline. No radio or intercom was needed to speed the word. These two mighty men, dressed nattily in store clothes, shoes shined, hats set just so, valises in hand, lingered on the threshold for a moment like two prominent bankers waiting for a commuter train." This pause allowed the crew to quickly "make the boat legal. The engineer knocked the grate bars off the safety valve, turned back the hand on the steam gauge to its honest reading, and gave the fire pump a shot of steam to make sure it worked. The mate threw half-empty paint cans in the paint locker and slammed the door on them, filled the fire buckets on the roof with water, and sent a sailor flying aloft to rid out from under the pilothouse the collection of junk which normally gravitated there. Meanwhile the captain, standing with the inspectors on the head of the boat, made a lot of polite talk, which he kept up, until presently the mate sauntered by and rapped a capstan-bar three thumps on the deck, river-Morse that the coast was clear."[80]

This riverboat kabuki play became rarer when in April 1853 federal statutes demanded that boilers be rigorously inspected, life-saving equipment furnished, hulls examined, and pilots and engineers licensed. Way reveals that by "a peculiar quirk of etiquette, steamboat captains were not subject to license until many years later. The title captain was a flowery exhalation [sic] backed up by no official document whatever. Anybody could be a captain who owned a boat and who had a swallow-tail coat and a silk plug hat." These new safety requirements provided many steamboat captains and operators

with an opportunity for high dudgeon and pompous protests. Way records that in April a group of them meeting in Cincinnati passed resolutions about safety measures, opining that "we regard the late Act of Congress as impolite, ridiculous and unnecessary, and that the encumberances [sic] now attached to steamboats, in the shape of life preservers, life boats, and inspectors, are incompatible with our skill as pilots and engineers, and at war with our ideas of humanity and common sense."[81]

Despite efforts to improve safety, the carnage continued, much of it tied to cotton lint. With hundreds of bales packed onto steamboats, hot smoke cascading from stacks overhead, and sparks flying, it seems incredible that any cotton boats survived. Fires could spread rapidly throughout the vessel and incinerate a steamer in a matter of minutes, resulting in dozens of persons maimed, burned to death, or drowned. McDermott calls steamboat travel "a world of trials and hazards you share in when voyaging on the Mississippi." Opportunities for mayhem abounded. Fires, crevasses, snags, sawyers, reefs, tornadoes, exploding boilers, collisions, and high water all did their share to sink vessels. Regardless of the cause, McDermott advises that "hardly a steamboat is in service for more than two or three years."[82] Though not often credited for steamboat problems, flooding led to difficulties as well. Hunter says that "Boats could be carried away and wrecked or stranded high on the shore; woodyards were swept away; paved waterfront landings were buried in mud; and the difficulty of making landings and transferring cargo brought business to a standstill."[83]

Though disasters abounded on Lower Mississippi rivers, steamboat travel maintained its sophisticated status throughout the 1850s, or so

---

[80]Way, *Horns*, 61.

[81]Way, *Horns*, 63.

[82]McDermott, xxiii.

[83]Hunter, 230.

some said. Others said differently. The naysayers included several celebrities, particularly British ones. Author Charles Dickens describes the river as a ditch of liquid mud and suggests that "it is well for society that this Mississippi, the renowned father of waters, had no children who take after him. It is the beastliest river in the world."[84] Another British writer, Frances Trollop, expresses her contempt for fellow passengers. "I would infinitely prefer sharing the apartment of a party of well-conditioned pigs."[85] Herman Melville shares his observations about fellow steamboat travelers with an acute eye for detail. "Men of business and men of pleasure; parlor men and backwoodsmen; farm hunters, and fame-hunters; heiress-hunters, gold-hunters, buffalo-hunters . . . happiness-hunters, truth-hunters, and still keener hunters after all these hunters. Fine ladies in slippers, and moccasined [sic] squaws; northern speculators and Eastern philosophers . . . Santa Fe traders in striped blankets, and Broadway bucks in cravats of cloth of gold; fine-looking Kentucky boatmen, and Japanese-looking Mississippi cotton planters, Quakers in full drab, and United States soldiers in full regimentals."[86]

One cannot help but wonder what these trenchant critics would have made of some entertainment that toured Arkansas waterways in 1858 aboard *Banjo* and *James Raymond*. The vessels carried Signor Carlos Donetti's Great Parisian Troup of Acting Monkeys, Dogs, and Goats. Despite a seemingly unmanageable cast, the December 25, 1858, edition

of the Fort Smith *Herald* gave their performance a rave review. "This is no humbug, for I have seen them and they can, and will do just what they say on their bills." Despite plentiful entertainment in New Orleans, during 1859 many people from that party town travelled to Hot Springs, Arkansas for $28 aboard the steamers *Irene* and *Red Wing*. An *Arkansas Gazette* reporter called Hot Springs the "only watering place in the South, if not in the whole country, which affords theatrical amusements to its visitors." The journalist admitted that crowds had thinned out somewhat, but not interest in the theater. It remained "in the full tide of successful experiment." He attributed that in part to Charles Paine, "jig dancer and Ethiopian delineator," doing whatever a delineator does.

Some Delta entertainment venues could be dangerous. Near the White River's mouth, Montgomery Point, Arkansas became a location where many large steamers switched cargoes and passengers to smaller boats headed up Delta rivers. It also provided a market for many vices and a den for thieves. Arkansas Governor Archibald Yell had a close call there. An *Arkansas Historical Quarterly* article shared his "personal account of an attempted robbery and possible murder on his person by cut-throats who operated in the thick cane-break jungle back of the warehouse and hotels which were built on the wharf. Gambling and skullduggery at Montgomery Point made old Napoleon's reputation pale in significance."[87]

---

[84]Charles Dickens's, *Pilgrim Edition of the Letters of Charles Dickens,* Vol. 3 (London: Oxford University Press, 1988), 194. This volume contains Dickens's letters from 1842 and 1843.

[85]Frances Trollop, *Domestic Manners of the Americans* (New York: Alfred A. Knopf, 1904), 16. Originally published in 1832, this book presents a lively portrait of early 19th century America as observed by a woman with keen insights.

[86]Herman Melville, *The Confidence Man: His Masquerade* (New York: Literary Classics of the United States, Inc., 1984), 848. Melville's name brings to mind a different type of boat, different body of water, and an elusive whale. This novel is a satire set on a New Orleans-bound riverboat. It debunks American idealism and paints a dark picture of a country being swallowed by illusions of progress.

[87]Dr. and Mrs. T. L Hodges, "Possibilities for the Archeologist and Historian in Eastern Arkansas," *Arkansas Historical Quarterly* 2:2 (June 1943), 161.

The *Chapmans Theatre* showboat. Tulane University Library.

A performance aboard the showboat *New Sensations*.

Entertainment on the River

River travel created several cultural icons, showboats being one of them. Though these attractions had become common by the 1850s, author Philip Graham credits William Chapman with launching at Pittsburgh, Pennsylvania the first "deliberately planned showboat" in 1831. Chapman and several family members "watched the small craft, no larger than a keelboat, slide off the ways and bob jerkily onto the Ohio."[88] Many of the troupe were born in England and there established reputations for turning in successful performances in a variety of roles. After arriving in America they advanced their careers in show business and decided that performing in a mobile theater might prove to be lucrative. From a stage at the stern and with candles for footlights, the shows went on. After docking at a village, two men went ashore to announce the performance schedule and price, typically 50 cents per ticket. However, sometimes they worked for gallons of fruit, sides of bacon, and pecks of potatoes. Shows often began with a drama, followed by a monologue, impersonations, and musical reviews with dancers. Since most audience members never had seen such an extravaganza, reviews tended to be favorable.

The Chapman plan included drifting down the Mississippi, stopping for one-night stands at places where audiences could be assembled. They intended to sell the boat at New Orleans, and if the trip proved successful, return to Pittsburgh, Pennsylvania and do it again. Graham says that sometimes they poled "up the wild Arkansas and the still wilder White River, where occasionally they had to use bird shot to repel ruffians who would have boarded them by force."[89] Despite such perils, the Chapmans began what became a river industry. Showboats soon grew in size and extravagance with sometimes spectacular entertainment. Many steamers had stage lights, orchestra pits, and offered melodramas, concerts, dancers, operas, self-improvement lectures, exhibitions of stuffed birds, circuses, and wax figures of the 12 apostles. Unfortunately some featured minstrel shows with demeaning black caricatures as well.

Many showboats plied rivers in the Delta, seeking to separate rubes from their money, but in some instances Arkansans sought to separate show people from their money. Graham indicates that at "such notorious spots" as the St. Francis River, men and women aboard showboats armed themselves with swords used in stage performances to repel "river robbers."[90] Despite their best efforts, some rough customers got on board, particularly in Arkansas, where "men came on board with a pistol in one pocket, a whiskey flask in the other, and long bowie knives sticking from their boots." Armed entertainers "at a given signal [were] prepared to defend the boat."[91]

Wittsburg, Arkansas on the St. Francis River probably was one of the most dangerous theater venues. The town began taking shape in the late 1840s and probably acquired its name from the Witt family. This riverside village became an ideal commercial location for trading with settlers along Crowley's Ridge. Steamboats delivered goods and carried out cotton, fur, and timber. The small town may have deserved its scurrilous reputation. At one point four retail liquor stores paid business taxes. The town council's responsibilities included prohibition of disorderly houses and licensing of sleight-of-hand

---

[88] Philip Graham, *Showboats. The History of an American Institution* (Austin: University of Texas Press, 1951), 9. Graham tells the story of this remarkable entertainment venue, from its first days until its last. Showboats ventured far and wide through frontier rivers. For the most part their audiences lacked sophistication, but not an appreciation for the sights they beheld. Performances were their opportunity to visit a colorful world of imagination, and Graham covers it from calliope to curtain call.

[89] Graham, 15.

[90] Graham, 6.

[91] Graham, 33.

performances. At its peak Wittsburg only had a few hundred residents, one of whom was Charles Carr until his execution by hanging in October 1878 after convicted of rape. Shotguns appear to have been the weapon of choice to settle town quarrels. A doctor named Crump was killed by a shotgun blast in a saloon one summer night in 1876. A fellow named Little died the same way. After a man named Redmond beat up one named Ferry, a shotgun round ended Redmond's life. The town died out by about 1890, but not entirely by shotgun blasts. Railroads killed the village when engineers laid their track to other locations.

Steamboat passengers occasionally participated in religious services, depicted in this drawing aboard *Ruth*, while headed down the Mississippi River. A. R. Waud, *Harpers Weekly* May 12, 1866.

All Aboard

Steamboat passengers represented all social classes, from high society to those on the bottom. An imaginary line between these two groups existed at the boiler deck. Between those who lived above the main deck and those who lived on it there was no equality. In this sense life on steamers was a southern world in miniature. Eliza Steele describes riverboat passage for an upper-class woman during summer travel. While aboard *Monsoon*, "ascending a stair-way you find yourself upon the guards, a walk extending all around the boat like a narrow piazza, from which several doors open into the rooms. The ladies cabin is handsomely furnished with every convenience, and in some instances with a piano. Above this is yet another deck called the hurricane deck. This is the best situation for viewing the scenery." During afternoons a "siesta is the fashion, and every one turns in his berth to take a nap. I did not follow this custom, as I was unwilling to lose any of the scenery, so that I usually stole out of my state room, like a mouse from its hole, and after a long look up and down the river, stole in again, the heat being too great to allow of a long stay.

"Our mornings on board are generally very social, the ladies sitting with the gentlemen of their party upon the guards, or gathering in groups with their work." However, as temperatures rose during the day, so did discomfort. One afternoon Steele became "oppressed with thirst and with heat, for the thermometer on board stood at ninety-six. I went into the ladies cabin in search of water, a jar of which filled with lumps of ice, was placed upon a marble table in one corner of the cabin. The ladies were all in their berths except two, who were using every means and appliance to keep themselves cool. They were each in a rocking chair kept in motion, their feet upon an ottoman, [which] made a table

for their books, while a large feather fan in one hand, and a lump of ice in another, were tolerable arms against the fire king." The lazy days Steele describes came to a sudden and unwelcome end on one occasion. "I left the cabin and walked out upon the shady side of the guards. I leaned over the railing and found the banjo player and his audience all in slumbering attitudes, or swinging in their hammocks, and everything denoted silence and repose. Suddenly a terrific and astounding bang, clang and clatter, as if the boat had been cracked to atoms. In a moment every one tumbled out and rushed upon the deck exclaiming, 'What's the matter?' The old Kentucky lady who had stepped out first, took her pipe from her mouth and said, quietly, 'It's only a log.' 'Oh, only a log; nothing but a log,' echoed from every mouth, and returning to their cabins they all stepped into their berths again. I looked around me in amazement. 'Madam,' said I, turning to the Kentucky woman, 'will you have the goodness to tell me what a log is.'"[92]

Given her lack of knowledge about logs, Steele appears to have been a rather genteel traveler. Steamboat operators took female passengers like her into consideration when designing accommodations for refined ladies. Builders located the ladies cabin at the rear of the boiler deck, as far as possible from heat and noise generated by engines. Partitions of some sort separated berths assigned to women and men to maintain propriety. Women typically enjoyed more elegant accommodations. Berths usually had small windows for light and ventilation. Some steamers provided large staterooms for entire families. Normally, servants slept on the saloon floor. During the early years of boating, washrooms adjoined both the women's and men's sections of the cabins. They contained tin basins with dirty river water and roller towels. According to

---

[92]Eliza Steele, *A Summer Journey in the West* (New York: J. S. Tayler & Co., 1840), 208-210; 212-213. At the urging of friends, Steele published her observations of a 4,000-mile summer tour starting in New York during the early 19th Century that included the Great Lakes; the Illinois, Mississippi, and Ohio rivers; and a return to New York via the Allegheny mountains.

Hunter, some washrooms provided one brush and comb, and "more than one traveler reported the presence of a community toothbrush"[93] Conditions improved by the 1850s when most staterooms had a washstand and some cabins had bathrooms with cold and hot water.

Protocol allowed husbands to sleep in the ladies cabin with their wives, and children slept there as well. Single men could enter that space during the day, but only when invited by a female passenger. Women had access to the men's cabin during daylight, but were never allowed in male staterooms. Gudmestad quotes one passenger, most likely a man, describing amusements in the ladies cabin as "nonsense, flirtation, and music."[94] The stream of flirtation flowed both ways, however. Bachelors visiting the ladies cabin flirted and displayed charming qualities popular in contemporary social rituals. If successful, they might win the hand of a belle for a turn on the promenade deck. Male activities in the men's cabin tended to be much different. Men often got drunk, gambled, cursed, spit tobacco, and displayed other bad habits. Steamers usually had rules of etiquette prominently posted that forbade unseemly behavior, but they tended to be ignored. Various rules attempting to govern male behavior aboard steamboats "were a tacit recognition of the difficulty that men had in restraining their baser impulses, says Gudmestad."[95]

Many woes beset unmarried couples caught traveling together with carnal knowledge. The Cincinnati *Gazette* on March 31, 1858, reported one example. A boat's officers discovered an unmarried couple "occupying the same berth. While the boat was held at a landing the next morning a number of the passengers compelled the young man to obtain a marriage license and then, before the journey up the river was resumed, escorted the couple to a minister and saw them properly married." Despite such exceptions, the "floating society was on the whole well behaved, surprisingly so perhaps in view of its diverse elements and the absence of many of the normal restraints on conduct. Steamboats running in most trades were outside the effective jurisdiction of state and local authorities." This situation invested the captain with some authority over manners and morals, aided by frontiersmen whose sense of justice stressed law and order.[96]

---

[93] Hunter 398.

[94] Gudmestad, 74.

[95] Gudmestad, 75.

[96] Hunter, 410-411.

Boats Built, Destroyed, or Noteworthy: 1850s

Admiral: made weekly trips from Memphis to several Arkansas locations—-Augusta, West Point, and Searcy—- during January 1859. The vessel helped bring about 1,200 persons to the White River Valley, more than half of them newcomers. (Huddleston, 51.)

Altoona: sternwheel packet (1853) lost at Montgomery Towhead in 1859 near the old mouth of the White River. (Way, 17.)

America: sidewheel packet (1849) snagged and sank on the St. Francis River in January 1857. (Way, 19.)

Arkadelphia City: sternwheel packet (1859) exploded at DeCeipher Shoals about 12 miles south of Little Rock shortly before the Civil War. The wife and baby of Captain W. A. Britton were "blown ashore unhurt." Unfortunately, five deckhands died. (Way, 29.)

B. M. Runyan: sidewheel packet (1858). It fatally snagged in July 1864 at Island No. 84 on the Mississippi River near Gaines Landing, Arkansas carrying soldiers headed north after their enlistments had expired. Estimates of lives lost ranged from more than 70 to more than 150. (Way, 35-36.)

Camden: sternwheel packet (1855) snagged and sank at Fulton, Arkansas in April 1857. (Way, 69.)

Caroline: steamer (1853) burned, killing about 45 persons in March 1854. A March edition of the Memphis *Weekly Appeal* reported the disaster. "The Memphis and White River packet *Caroline* is burned. She took fire in White River, about twenty miles above the mouth . . . and was totally destroyed." Captain John R. Trice, "with a nobleness deserving a better fate, remained at his post, and with a coolness and judgment remarkable under

Re-creation of newspaper headline describing the loss of *Caroline.* Captain Vernon Rees Downs Papers, Memphis Public Library.

the circumstances, placed the boat upon the only spot where the passengers could have been saved. The scene that followed is indescribable. About 15 persons took possession of the yawl, and crowded into it, sunk it, and everyone perished." After water filled its stern, *Caroline* went down. "In about a minute she reappeared and raised herself out of the water, bow foremost, about twenty-five feet. She then broke in two and settled down gradually until she was entirely out of sight."

Clermont No. 2: sank in December 1851 near Augusta, Arkansas after striking a snag; apparently 22 of 26 deck passengers died. (Huddleston, 31.)

Comet: made its maiden voyage up the White River in December 1857, but after that trip switched to St. Francis River trade. (Huddleston, 40.)

Conway: sternwheel packet built during 1859 at Lewisburg, Arkansas. The vessel went down at Badgett Landing in Arkansas during December 1860; later raised. (Way, 110.)

Cotton Plant: sidewheel packet (1846) burned at Napoleon, Arkansas during May 1852. (Way, 113.)

Crescent City: Stewart-Abernathy believes that "A key event in the development of towing may have been an 1854 trip down the Mississippi" by this vessel. Four coal barges were pushed rather than pulled, which lessened maneuvering difficulties. Sidewheelers previously pulled barges or lashed them beside the steamer, which decreased a vessel's agility and speed. The shipment of three commodities helped keep many Mississippi towboats busy: coal from Pennsylvania; forest products from the Upper Mississippi, and grain shipped from St. Louis. (Stewart-Abernathy, 49-50.)

Dardanelle: sternwheel packet (1856). One of at least two vessels with the same name, this version snagged and sank at Pine Bluff, Arkansas in February 1859. (Way, 120.)

Davenport: sidewheel ferry (1855) pressed into Union service during 1864. It went down in the Arkansas River at the head of Evan's Bar above Little Rock. (Way, 120.)

Defender: sternwheel packet (1855) snagged and destroyed in April 1860 at Laconia, Arkansas; five lives lost. (Way, 122.)

D. H. Morton: sidewheel packet (1856) loaded with hay and grain burned at Gay's Landing near the head of Prairie Bend in the Arkansas River during March 1859. (Way, 117.)

Diligent: sidewheel packet (1859) used by the Union Army in the 1860s to transport sick and wounded men. It struck a snag and sank at Helena, Arkansas in January 1865. (Way, 129.)

Dispatch: inaugurated mail service to Batesville, Arkansas in October 1850. The vessel's schedule called for it to leave Batesville each Saturday morning and travel to Napoleon, Arkansas where it would connect with Mississippi River mail boats and return to Batesville within the week. That following December it ran into a snag and went under about 30 miles

above the mouth of the White River. The sidewheel packet *J.B. Gordon* (1848) and *Santa Fe* replaced *Dispatch*, but *J.B. Gordon* sank approximately seven miles below Batesville in May 1851. (Huddleston, 23.)

Dr. Buffington: sternwheel packet (1857) lost on the White River in December 1862. (Way, 130.)

Ella: sternwheel packet (1854) struck a snag and destroyed in December 1865 on the Arkansas River near Little Rock. (Way, 145.)

E.M. Ryland: entered Jacksonport-Memphis trade. The steamer made a stop at Des Arc, Arkansas in September 1859, and the captain invited citizens to a dance aboard his vessel. A September 14, 1859, Des Arc *Citizen* provided a florid account of the affair. "The young, the gay, and the beautiful were there, and they moved in the graceful mazes of dance. We were reminded of earlier years and the bewitching snares that twine around the hearts of the young."

Exchange: sternwheel packet (1852). Despite the captain's claim that his vessel "draws but 13 inches and freight will be delivered without detention," it snagged and sank during January 1858 in the White River. (Way, 157.)

Forest City: sidewheel packet (1851) starting in 1857 handled mail for Napoleon-Vicksburg route. (Way, 169.)

Forest Rose: sternwheel packet (1852) boilers exploded in March 1857 while upbound from New Orleans to the Arkansas River. Between six and 14 persons died, including the seven-year-old son of Captain Allen. The disaster happened about two miles below Napoleon, Arkansas and "the sound was heard there." (Way, 169.)

Fox: sternwheel packet built at Little Rock during 1855. Fire destroyed the vessel above a raft on the Red River during March 1861. Builders at Little Rock constructed a ferry named *Fox* in 1876. (Way, 171.)

Garden City: sidewheel packet (1853) burned in January 1855 below Napoleon, Arkansas. (Way, 177.)

General Bem: sidewheel packet (1849). A Jacksonport, Arkansas newspaper reviewed the efficiency of this boat: "The *General Bem* came up with the mail on Friday — she will be up again as soon as she can. The mailboats of late transport the mails with the speed of lightning — B-U-G-S! — in a walk." (Huddleston, 23.) A report in the Memphis *Weekly Appeal* on January 7, 1852, proved equally critical. "This speed reveals the velocity of a snail's gallop." Way reports that the much maligned vessel hit a snag and went down at Walnut Bend in the Arkansas River during January 1854; ten persons died. (Way, 179)

General Pike: sidewheel packet (1851). On this vessel's first voyage down the Mississippi River several gamblers were on board "who filched a goodly amount of money from one of the passengers," according to the Des Arc *Citizen* on December 11, 1858. "Whether the money was lost by gambling or some con game is unclear; the report revealed only that the passenger thought he had a sure thing in betting against their tricks." Fortunately for the victim, several passengers and steamboat officers intervened and forced the slickers to return his money. After the steamer proceeded on its journey, it stopped at isolated points along the river where the "culprits were deposited singly to bemoan their fate." On another trip the vessel made some good news by undertaking a rescue mission reported in the May 25, 1859, edition of the *Citizen*. As the steamer passed Des Arc, Arkansas the boat's crew rescued a family from a house where they had been trapped for some time by high water. The steamer's passengers passed several complimentary resolutions commending the boat and its officers "to those who may wish to travel with comfort, pleasure, and in safety."

Grapeshot: sternwheel packet (1855) snagged and lost at Van Buren, Arkansas in June 1859. (Way, 197.)

Grosse Tete: sidewheel packet (1858) converted into a Confederate gunboat named *Maurepas*. The crew scuttled it in the White River near St. Charles, Arkansas during June 1862 to obstruct the channel. (Way 201.)

Hickman: sidewheel packet (1855) burned in March 1860 below Little Rock; two lives lost. (Way, 215.)

Interchange: sternwheel packet (1854) hit a snag and sank at Newport, Arkansas in October 1860. (Way, 225.)

Isaac Shelby: sternwheel packet (1856) snagged and lost at Swan Lake, Arkansas in June 1860. (Way, 226.)

James Laughlin: sternwheel packet (1853) servicing Napoleon, Arkansas, the White River, and Memphis. It sank at Memphis in September 1856; six lives lost. (Way, 240.)

Jefferson: sidewheel packet (1851) ran from Batesville, Arkansas to Memphis. It went down after snagging at Pine Bluff, Arkansas during February 1852. Way mentions eight boats with this name. (Way, 244.)

Jesse Lazear: sternwheel packet (1854) snagged and lost in the White River during January 1858. (Way, 246.)

J. H. Done: sternwheel packet (1854) worked an Arkansas River-Cincinnati route in 1861 and sank at Scotia on the Upper Arkansas during 1864. (Way, 231.)

Joe Wilson: sidewheel ferry (1852) exploded at Columbus, Arkansas in January 1853. (Way, 249.)

John Briggs: light-draft packet (1856) that could carry freight in water only four feet deep, according to its owners. The vessel worked Jacksonport-New Orleans trade. (Huddleston, 41.)

George H. Devol: Quintessential Riverboat Gambler

George H. Devol. From Devol's autobiography.

Many riverboats on the Lower Mississippi displayed signs such as, "Games for money strictly forbidden." They were mostly ignored. Hunter says that in 1855 "one might have seen from four to six gambling tables stretched out in the main cabin in full blast for money. The reason boats went one eye blind on this business was because the professional gamblers were quite a percentage of the passengers, very liberal in paying for the best rooms, tipping the cabin boys, and [were] good liberal customers at the bar." Steamers held plenty of marks—-"planters and farmers returning from market with proceeds of crops in their pocket, emigrants moving west with much of their resources reduced to cash, and merchants with funds for the purchase of new stocks." These passengers "offered rich plums to him who could successfully shake the tree."[97]

George H. Devol was one of the best at shaking the tree. This excerpt from his autobiography describes how he departed Natchez, Mississippi on *Tippecanoe*, "a snug little boat, running in the cotton trade between Natchez and Princeton. As gamblers are accustomed to do, soon after going on board, I endeavored to ascertain what the prospects were for the game. The usual way of doing this is by going around and forming acquaintances among the players in a friendly game of whist, eucher, boston, seven-up, or old-sledge. This is done to draw in the unsuspecting, to see who plays, and what amount of money they carry upon their persons." Devol describes one example of cheating an unsuspecting sucker. "I ran him out three Queens and helped myself to three Kings." After pushing the man to bet more and more money on his queens, "hands were shown and the portly man wilted like a leaf before a November blast."[98]

---

[97]Hunter, 408-409

[98]George H. Devol, *Forty Years a Gambler on the Mississippi* (Cincinnati: Devol and Haines, 1887), 148. Born in Ohio during 1829, this greatest of the riverboat gamblers ran away from home when ten years old to work as a steamboat cabin boy. By the age of 14 he could stack a deck of cards and found his true calling. During a long career on the river, Devol fleeced many suckers. Fortunately he could fight as well as he cheated at cards and lived long enough to enjoy his ill-gotten wealth.

Devol's gambling trickery almost cost his life when he stopped in Arkansas. He says that "Helena and Napoleon, Ark., were two towns where it was not safe for any man to do the bluff act, for they would kill him just to see him kick. I won some money from one of Helena's killers at one time on board a steamer, and he set up a big kick; but as he was alone, he was like all men of his class—-a coward. I well knew if he caught me on his ground I would get the worst of it, so I resolved never to give him a chance; but one evening I was compelled to get off at Helena, as things had gotten a little too warm for me on board the boat, and I thought I would run the risk of the killers rather than give up the money I had won at that time."

Unfortunately for Devol, while on his way to a hotel for supper he met the so-called coward that he had bested. Devol waited until the steamer he planned to board arrived at the pier, but as he started out of the hotel the clerk told him that a gambler, Devol as it turned out, had beaten one of the "worst men in the country on a boat, and he was down at the landing with a crowd of his roughs, waiting to do him up." Thus warned, Devol called for a carriage to deliver him at the gangway, but other gamblers "left the hotel and started for the landing before the boat came in. The killers jumped on the poor gamblers supposing of course that I was among them. They beat them up fearfully, and came near killing one of them. During the excitement I was driven to the plank and jumped out, and was on board before any one recognized me. When the killers learned that I had given them the slip, they were determined to board the boat and get me; but the mate got his crew on the guards and would not let any of them on board. I think that was one of my close calls."[99]

A game underway. From Devol's autobiography.

[99]Devol, 236-237.

John Raine: The *Louisville Courier Journal* reported on August 8, 1859, the fate of a man caught stealing on this vessel as it headed north from New Orleans along the Delta. After about 30 passengers were robbed they formed a committee to search suspects. All but one submitted, and he jumped overboard, but was overtaken by the crew in a yawl. The victims found stolen property on him, and he was "most terribly whipped, and chased from the stern to the bow of the boat, which was again under way going up river. The fellow, rendered desperate by the unmerciful whippings . . . again jumped overboard." This time he escaped.

J. Morrisett: During January 1857 a hard freeze made the White River impassable, stranding *J. Morrisett, Louisa,* and *Editor. J. Morrisett* later collided with a snag and sank just above Jacksonport, Arkansas. (Huddleston, 40.)

Julia Dean: A brawl occurred on *Julia Dean* in October 1854. The vessel departed Memphis with about 100 Irish deck passengers headed downriver to work on Mississippi River levees. At the mouth of the White River the steamer ran aground and remained stuck for about 24 hours. To kill time, deck passengers threw a party with alcohol. The festivities degenerated into a brawl. To help regain control, the wily Captain Bateman persuaded about 40 celebrants to go ashore by telling them that they had reached their destination. After *Julia Dean* resumed its journey, crewmen attempted to subdue the remaining troublemakers, but violence erupted again. Before the fighting Irishmen were overcome, male cabin passengers had to assist the crew. (Huddleston, 39.)

Julia Roane: sternwheel packet (1859) built at Little Rock and burned there in September 1863. (Way, 261.)

Justice: An article in the July 1, 1855, Memphis *Daily Appeal* indicated that only this vessel remained on the White River after all others migrated for the summer season. "The *Justice,* last of the Mohicans, or rather the only boat left in the White River trade, will leave this port on her return trip Thursday next."

Key West: sternwheel packet (1857). The vessel operated part of the year in northern waters and some months in Arkansas River-New Orleans trade. During December 1862 it burned at Van Buren, Arkansas. (Way, 271.)

Leon: sternwheel packet (1859) owned by a Van Buren, Arkansas stock company and used in the Arkansas River. It snagged and sank at Barnum, Arkansas in March 1864. (Way, 282.)

Luella: sternwheel packet (1850) lost on the White River during September 1855 after colliding with *Jesse Lazear.* (Way, 298.)

Mary L. Dougherty: sidewheel packet (1853) in White River –Memphis trade lost on the White River during December 1854. (Way, 313.)

May Queen: sternwheel packet (1850) collapsed a flue on the Arkansas River in February 1852; 12 persons killed and seven badly wounded. (Way, 317.)

Pennsylvania: sidewheel packet (1854) exploded its boilers at Ship Island between Helena, Arkansas and Commerce, Missouri in June 1858. Twain mentions this catastrophe in *Life on the Mississippi* "inasmuch as Twain's younger brother Henry was scalded fatally." U.S. Customs set the death toll at 20, but other accounts estimated 154 persons lost or missing. (Way, 367.)

Pine Bluff: sternwheel packet (1859) ran Arkansas River-New Orleans trade until burned in 1866 at Pittsburgh, Pennsylvania while loading out for the Arkansas River. (Way, 372.)

Pitser Miller: exploded at the mouth of the White River in January 1852; three lives lost. (Lloyd, 293.)

Pocahontas: sidewheel packet (1849) almost destroyed while pulling away from a Dardanelle, Arkansas woodyard in March 1852 when two flues

Randall and another steamer stuck on a White River sandbar. Lyon College.

blew out. After an explosion the boat caught fire, but officers and crew saved the steamer. Unfortunately 18 persons were scalded, and eight of them died the following morning. (Lloyd, 258.)

Pontchartrain: sidewheel packet (1859) converted into a Confederate gunboat and destroyed by U. S. *General Price* in September 1863 near Little Rock. (Way, 375.)

Quapaw: sternwheel packet (1857) transported Seminoles from Florida to Fort Smith, Arkansas. The steamer snagged and went down in February 1861 near Little Rock. Another *Quapaw*, a sternwheel snagboat, was constructed at Little Rock in 1893. U.S. engineers used this vessel on the White, Black, and Current rivers. (Way, 380.)

Rainbow: sidewheel packet (1854) burned about 10 miles above Napoleon, Arkansas in November 1857 with 75 or more lives lost. (Way, 387.)

Red Wing: sternwheel packet (1856) hit a snag and sank at Smith's cutoff in May 1860 during Little Rock-Memphis trade. (Way, 390.)

Return: In August 1859 it smashed into a snag. The object knocked a hole in the boat's side, and it sank in 10 minutes; no loss of life. (Huddleston, 41.)

Romeo: sidewheel packet (1850) snagged and lost at Champagnolle, Arkansas in December 1851. (Way, 401.)

Rough and Ready: sternwheel packet (1856) lost in a collision with *Monongahela* at Napoleon, Arkansas during 1858. (Way, 403.)

Sangamon: sidewheel packet (1853) snagged and lost at St. Charles, Arkansas in February 1856. (Way, 419.)

Sam Hale: One of northern Arkansas's most prominent citizens, Colonel John Ringgold drowned after falling overboard in January 1857. He died only 30 feet from the shore about ten miles above Clarendon, Arkansas, according to the February 5, 1857, Memphis *Daily Appeal*.

St. Joseph: This vessel's demise took place at the mouth of the Arkansas River during January 1850. A sidewheel packet (1846) bound from New Orleans to St. Louis, Missouri, it was running side by side with *South America* when the accident occurred. A larboard boiler of *St. Joseph* exploded, setting fire to the boat. The explosion instantly killed a boy at the engine and mortally wounded the second engineer. Lloyd describes a horribly wounded Missouri passenger. "He lingered in great agony for twenty-four hours, having every particle of skin peeled from his body. It is believed that eight or ten persons were drowned."

(Lloyd, 259.) Given that both steamers were side by side and an exploding boiler caused this catastrophe, one might assume that a race was underway.

Thomas P. Ray: The December 27, 1854, Memphis *Daily Appeal* reported a disaster that befell this steamer. "We learn from a young friend who has just returned to the city from a visit to Little Rock that he passed *T. P Ray* in White River where she is waiting for a section of steam pipe to be sent from Memphis. It is thought that those soldiers who were badly scalded will recover. The five who were lost were probably blown over board and drowned." During spring 1856 high winds separated this boat from its moorings at Batesville, Arkansas, and the steamer sank.

Umpire No. 2: sternwheel packet (1850) snagged and lost above Little Rock in August 1854. (Way, 462.)

Violet: sternwheel packet (1856) burned at Van Buren, Arkansas in December 1862. (Way, 470.)

W. H. Langley: sternwheel packet (1856) began White River-Napoleon-Memphis trade in 1858. Confederates seized the vessel during spring 1861 for use as a transport, but Union forces captured it at Memphis in June 1862. (Way, 499.)

Steamboats Amid Strife

Delta steamboats reached full throttle in the 1850s, but the Civil War brought many of them to an abrupt stop. On May 6, 1861, by a vote of 69 to one, members of an Arkansas convention adopted an ordinance of secession. Civil War leaders on both sides of the conflict recognized the Mississippi River's strategic value. Union commanders realized that by seizing the river they would possess a great natural highway and deny the Confederacy fertile resources in Arkansas, Louisiana, and Texas. For two years and three months after the fall of Fort Sumter at Charleston, South Carolina both sides strove to control the big river. This struggle for domination eventually would be decided at Vicksburg, Mississippi in July 1863.[100] Given the region's extensive waterways, each side calculated that the contest hinged on naval power. Along with building ironclads from scratch, military commanders turned steamboats into gunboats. Other commercial vessels became rams after alterations to their bows. Mortar boats mounted 13-inch mortars, and tugboats pulled them from one engagement to the next. Federals and Confederates commandeered vessels when possible and stripped off everything topside to add guns and ramparts plated with iron. Though plating on Confederate vessels tended to be heavier than on northern ships, they had several weaknesses: poor construction, inferior armament, and undependable machinery.[101] Confederate seizure of pre-war steamers became especially important since southerners lacked extensive manufacturing resources available to the North.

Conflict on Arkansas's side of the Mississippi River began before secession. In April 1861, Rebels at Napoleon, Arkansas became alarmed about news that federal authorities in Cincinnati, Ohio seized lead and powder being shipped to Memphis and New Orleans. They mounted cannons on the riverbank and forced boats bound up the Mississippi River to land for inspection. Militia fired on *Westmoreland* when the captain refused to turn over its cargo, killing one passenger and wounding another.[102] In a similar incident, Pine Bluff, Arkansas militiamen took over *Silver Wave* after word spread that the boat carried military and medical supplies for forts in Indian Territory. A search turned up no weapons or ammunition, but raiders found medical materials and commandeered them.

Though most Delta targets tended to be relatively easy prey for Union forces under General U. S. Grant, difficulties in conquering Vicksburg, Mississippi included protection of his Mississippi River supply lines. To maintain them he needed to eliminate constant sniping from shore, including along Arkansas rivers. By 1862, Rebel bushwhackers operated along the entire western side of the Mississippi River, says author Robert R. Mackey, "with Arkansas as the central base of operations for these elements."[103] Guerillas killed federal troops on boats, ambushed transports, and burned supply ships. To combat these marauders the Union war department established an unusual military unit, the Mississippi Marine Brigade. It consisted of eight transports equipped for rapid unloading of

---

[100]Francis Vinton Greene, *Campaigns of the Civil War: The Mississippi* (Edison, N. J.: Castle Books, 2002), 2. Greene draws upon official war records to describe Mississippi River campaigns rather than what he calls personal recollections. In addition to the Union's capture of the Mississippi River's big prizes—-Memphis, Vicksburg, New Orleans—-the author covers less momentous river battles such as Arkansas Post in January 1863 and Helena in July 1863.

[101]Greene, 10.

[102]DeBlack, 26.

[103]Robert R. Mackey, *The Uncivil War. Irregular Warfare in the Upper South, 1861-1865* (Norman: University of Oklahoma Press, 2004), 55. Mackey outlines the southern strategy for waging irregular warfare across an entire region, discusses the complex military issues involved, identifies the northern response, and explains the outcome.

This engraving depicts the effects of a deadly shot that disabled the ironclad *Mound City* in the center. Scuttled vessels *Eliza G, Mary Patterson,* and *Maurepas* are upriver. *Harper's Weekly*, July 12, 1862.

The Most Deadly Shot

Despite the Union's relatively low casualty counts while conquering most Delta targets compared to battles in northern Virginia, one federal assault caused an inordinate number of losses aboard a steamer. In June 1862 a flotilla consisting of *Mound City, St. Louis, Lexington,* and *Conestoga,* along with transports carrying troops, steamed into the White River. Their primary objective was destruction of gun emplacements at St. Charles, Arkansas. The attack succeeded without serious challenge according to Greene, until a shot "penetrated the casement of the *Mound City* and exploded the steam-drum. Many of the crew perished outright, others were frightfully scalded, and some jumped overboard and were drowned. Out of 175 people on board, only 35 escaped uninjured."[104] After observing this destruction,

a Union colonel described the actions of some Confederates. "The crew were seen from the shore to spring from the port holes into the river. Scarcely had they done so before a party of the enemy's sharpshooters descended the bluffs and under the cover of fallen timber on the river bank commenced murdering those who were struggling in the water, and also firing upon those in our boats sent to pick them up. At the same time another party of the enemy, concealed in the timber on the opposite bank of the river, pursued the same barbarous course."[105] Union gunboats achieved a measure of revenge that month when they attacked Memphis and crippled several Confederate vessels. The fatally damaged Confederate steamers *General Jeff Thompson* and *General P.T. Beauregard* went down on the Arkansas side of the Mississippi River.

---

[104]Greene, 17-18.

[105]Charles E. Pearson, Michael Tuttle, and Michael Krivor, "Survey for Submerged Cultural and Natural Resources, White River Navigation Maintenance, Arkansas, Desha, and Prairie Counties, Arkansas," Final Report (Baton Rouge, Coastal Environments, Inc., 2004), 16. This report focuses on navigation history, archaeological efforts, historic properties, and cultural resources in these counties along the White River.

artillery, men, and mounts; a hospital boat; several steam tugs; coal barges, and five small steamers. The unit contained about 1,200 soldiers "organized in a regiment of mule-mounted infantry, two cavalry squadrons, and a battery of howitzers."[106] Commanded by Brigadier General Alfred W. Ellet, the force developed features that would become standard tactics in anti-guerilla warfare, including rapid response, mobility, and superior fire power. Unfortunately for Arkansans, Union tactics included putting the torch to homes and villages believed to support guerillas.

While irregular warfare continued, a significant engagement joining the firepower of warships and infantry occurred at Arkansas Post. Aboard *Forest Queen*, Union General William T. Sherman wrote a letter in January 1863 to General H. W. Halleck proposing to move "our entire force in concert with the [U. S. Navy] gunboats to the Arkansas, which is now in boating condition, and reduce the Post of Arkansas, where seven thousand of the enemy are entrenched and threaten this river. One vessel, the *Blue Wing*, has been captured by the enemy, and with that enemy on our rear and flank our communications would at all times be endangered."[107] Halleck agreed, as did Admiral David Porter, so federal troops commanded by General John A. McClernand began moving upriver using transports guarded by Porter's naval squadron consisting of the following vessels: *DeKalb* with 13 guns; *Cincinnati*, 13 guns; *Louisville*, 13 guns; *Black Hawk*, 8 guns; *Lexington*, 7 guns; *Rattler*, 6 guns; *Glide*, 6 guns, and the ram *Monarch*.

On January 9, 1863, Union forces came within sight of Arkansas Post, designated Fort Hindman by Confederates. The four-sided fort stood on a bluff about 25 feet above the river. Trenches protected the garrison of approximately 5,000 men commanded by General T. J. Churchill. He possessed only a small number of artillery pieces, soon silenced by Union gunners. After federal commanders positioned their troops for an assault, Porter's warships opened fire on the vastly outgunned defenders. Federal barrages soon silenced Confederate artillery. Along with naval gunfire, Union field artillery helped crush the fort's defenses. Despite this intense bombardment, Confederates at first vigorously contested a Union infantry assault. However, a mistaken belief that Churchill ordered a surrender caused some defenders to raise a white flag, and Fort Hindman capitulated. Union gunboats reported only 31 killed and wounded in the engagement, though Federals had infantry casualties. Devastating fire by naval gunners probably saved the lives of many Union soldiers.[108]

The scarcity of momentous battles in the Delta did not signify a lack of ongoing conflict. Whether called partisan rangers or bushwhackers, southern irregulars continually hampered use of waterways without being lured into a stand-up fight. Author Leo E. Huff says that "the two most famous Confederate guerilla bands, or independent companies, that operated on the Mississippi near Memphis were those led by captains James H. McGhee and Joseph F. Barton." Their units contained many pilots and riverboat men and primarily plundered federal steamers. The companies did not mistreat prisoners or kill civilians, as did other guerillas, and they were under the "direct orders" of Confederate General T. C. Hindman.[109] While leading his rangers during January and February 1863, McGhee captured and torched three Union steamers and sank 12 coal barges. When *Jacob Musselman* docked at Hopefield, Arkansas, partisans captured the boat. They ordered the steamer to proceed upriver to where McGhee and about 60 guerillas waited.

---

[106]Mackey, 56

[107]Greene, 83.

[108]Greene, 86.

[109]Leo E. Huff, "Guerillas, Jayhawkers and Bushwhackers in Northern Arkansas During the Civil War," *Arkansas Historical Quarterly* 24: 2 (Summer 1965), 133.

Arkansas snipers preparing to fire on a riverboat. State Historical Society of Missouri.

Union Fort Curtis at Helena, Arkansas. Library of Congress.

They plundered the steamer and used it to capture a passing flatboat filled with livestock. Also that month, McGhee and about 33 men boarded *Grampus No. 2*, looted and burned it after releasing its crew. They also destroyed coal barges towed by the steamer. Their success continued in February when McGhee's men captured *Hercules* near a ferry landing at Hopefield, Arkansas when the boat towing seven coal barges tied up because of fog. Guerillas killed a deck hand when he attempted to run, plundered and burned the boat and took crewmen inland to their camp. They released their captives unharmed the next morning.[110]

Among the Delta's villages and landings, Helena, Arkansas became a serious problem for Confederates. The Union took the port in July 1862, and Confederates planned to take it back in July 1863. The town served as an important supply depot for Grant's Vicksburg campaign. After Confederate generals schemed and vacillated, their forces finally

set out piecemeal for Helena amid black gnats and pouring rain. When the commanding officer there, Major General Benjamin M. Prentiss, concluded that his forces faced an upcoming assault he prepared formidable defensive positions. The Union commander requested naval support and got the tinclad *Tyler*, the ram *General Bragg*, and tinclad *Hastings*.[111] Unfortunately for Prentiss, *Tyler* was at Memphis undergoing repairs, and on June 29 *General Bragg* also went to the city for repairs. Until July 2, only *Hastings* remained at Helena, and that steamer headed upriver when *Tyler* returned. Thus Prentiss had only one warship to support his troops. Fortunately for Federals, the Confederate attack proved to be ragged and ineffectual. Additionally, attackers faced imposing terrain and galling federal cannon fire. *Tyler* contributed to the repulse as well with effective gunnery. Confederate forces withdrew, but fearing another attack, Prentiss dispatched *Tycoon* to Memphis with prisoners and an appeal for reinforcements. The gunboat

---

[110]Huff, 133-134.

[111]Edwin C. Bearss, "The Battle of Helena, July 4, 1863," *Arkansas Historical Quarterly* 20:3 (Autumn 1961), 268.

Covington soon arrived, and the following day a transport, *General Anderson*, carrying Illinois infantrymen. Edwin C. Bearss declares that "the battle of Helena was the last effort on the part of the Confederates to retain control of a strong point on the Mississippi River, and to make a diversion in favor of Vicksburg." It ended in a disaster "and to some extent a discreditable defeat."[112]

Fed up with constant sniping from the Arkansas shoreline, Union forces destroyed many towns and plantations in 1863 from southern Missouri to northern Louisiana. Hopefield, Arkansas's turn came on February 19. Accused by Federals of sheltering partisans, the Arkansas town's residents received an hour to gather their belongings and leave. Union troops then burned it down. While being transported on a federal steamboat taking him north to a prisoner of war camp a Confederate prisoner observed the destruction he saw along the Delta and later wrote about it. "On the west bank of the Mississippi, extending from the mouth of the White River to this point [Helena], evidence innumerable why we should love the glorious Union, no less than five hundred blackened walls and lone chimneys are standing as monuments to departed civilized warfare."[113] Confederate General Joseph Shelby's cavalry also proved to be an ongoing threat to Union steamers in the Delta, particularly during summer 1864. In June a Union soldier, Orville Gillet, made this diary entry with respect to one of Shelby's conquests. "Rebels took *Gunboat 26*, 35 miles below here on the White River. The fleet started again for Little Rock but was obliged to return for the rebs had the river."[114] Shelby gathered up another prize from the White River. The gunboat *Queen City*, guarding the river at Clarendon, Arkansas, became a target, and DeBlack explains what happened. From about 200 yards, Confederates "opened up on the *Queen City* with small arms and four cannon. After twenty minutes of intense fire, the gunboat ran up a white flag. Some members of the crew escaped by jumping overboard and swimming to the opposite bank, but the captain and the remaining members of the crew were taken prisoner."[115] Confederates stripped the crippled vessel of guns, ammunition, and supplies before blowing it up. In retaliation *Tyler* and two more Union warships bombarded the guerillas, causing their withdrawal. Federal forces then burned down much of Clarendon.

Though Confederates did not give up the fight, when Vicksburg fell to the Union in July 1863 so did southern hopes of denying the Union control of the Mississippi River. During the war's waning months the Union continued to garrison towns along Delta rivers, and federal gunboats seized numerous vessels. In the last half of 1864 they pressed many White River steamboats into Union service. Among them: *John D. Perry, David Tatum, Sunny South, Silver Wave, Belle Peoria*, and *Commercial*. Federals used these vessels primarily as troop transports. Despite such seizures, some commercial steamers continued to work the White River during winter 1864-1865, including *Fanny Ogden, M.S. Mepham, Emma No. 2, William Wallace, Sunny South, Kate Hart, Curlew, Rose Hambleton, May Duke, War Eagle, Albert Pearce, Ella, Liberty No. 2, Citizen, St. Cloud, Belle Peoria, Lady, Mattie, W. Butler, Rebecca*, and *Rowena*.[116] However, by that time the war had deprived the Delta of items to buy, sell, or eat, except the bitter fruits of defeat.

---

[112]Bearss, 292-293.

[113]William W. Heartstill, *Fourteen Hundred and 91 Days* (Marshall, Texas), 101.

[114]Ted R. Worley, editor, "Diary of Lieutenant Orville Gillet," *The Arkansas Historical Quarterly* 17: 2 (Summer 1958), 164-165.

[115]DeBlack, 118.

[116]Huddleston, 63-65.

Boats Built, Destroyed, or Noteworthy: 1860s

Acacia: sternwheel packet (1856) seized by Confederates in 1861, but recaptured by Union forces at Memphis during 1862. Approximately 25 miles above Helena, Arkansas in August 1862 the vessel hit a snag, causing 40 deaths. *Conway* and *William H. Brown* rescued survivors. Way indicates that *Acacia* may have been involved in moving contraband cotton for the benefit of Union officers. In some loss reports, this vessel is erroneously identified as *Acacia Cottage*, another sternwheel packet built in 1857. (Way, 4, 496.)

Adams: In April 1864 the federal steamers *Adams* and *Chippewa*, loaded with provisions for Union General Frederick Steele's Red River expedition, departed Little Rock for Pine Bluff, Arkansas. They collided approximately 20 miles below Little Rock, sinking *Adams* and seriously crippling *Chippewa*.[117]

Ad Hine: sternwheel packet (1860) went down during February 1864 in the Arkansas River near Pine Bluff, Arkansas. (Way, 5.)

Agnes: sternwheel packet (1864) made trips between the White River and St. Louis, Missouri, but hit a snag and sank roughly ten miles below Vicksburg, Mississippi in March 1869. (Way, 7.)

A.H Sevier: sternwheel packet (1860) went down in the Arkansas River near Pine Bluff, Arkansas during December 1860. *Cedar Rapids* steamed to the rescue, but sank at Douglas, Arkansas on the Arkansas River. After *Frontier City* recovered salvage from the two wrecked vessels, it went under as well. (Way, 1.)

Aid: sidewheel ferry (1860) destroyed on the St. Francis River in January 1861 after striking a snag. (Way, 7.)

Argonaut No. 2: sternwheel packet (1862) seized at Cairo, Illinois during June 1864 by Union troops for war service. Sent up the White River on this steamer, a federal soldier described the region as a place "where Rebels are as thick as blackberries. Got to Duvalls [sic] Bluff to find ten other packets awaiting turn to unload cargo there." Way cites the federal trooper's observation that "the country below the Bluff 'abounds with frogs, snakes, wolves, bears, etc. and the river is full of fish.'" In December 1866 while lost in fog on the Ohio River this boat struck the Indiana shore and sank. (Way, 27.)

Argos: sternwheel packet (1864). According to the *Pittsburgh Commercial* on March 26, 1864, this "light draught boat" operated between Pittsburgh, Pennsylvania and Morgantown, West Virginia. However, it sank at Batesville, Arkansas in July 1871.

Arkansas Traveler: sternwheel packet (1856) snagged and lost at Pine Bluff, Arkansas in March 1860; one person killed. (Way, 30.)

A. W. Quarrier: departed Clarendon, Arkansas in June 1861 carrying Confederate troops to north Arkansas via the St. Francis River (Krivor, Final Report, Vol. I, 97.)

Belle Lee: built in 1868 and initially commanded by Captain T. P. Leathers. Not long after completion it caused a dust-up between Leathers and Captain John W. Cannon, who accused the former of a charter violation and rate cutting. The November 14, 1868, New Albany (Indiana) *Commercial* reported one consequence of this disagreement. "Capt. John W. Cannon and Capt. Tom Leathers, we are informed, indulged in a knock-down at New Orleans Saturday. Capt. Cannon had the best of the fight, so our information states." Despite some success, creditors foreclosed on the boat and sold it at auction. New owners enlarged its hull and named the steamer *Mary Bell.*

---

[117]Ira Don Richards, "The Battle of Poison Spring," *Arkansas Historical Quarterly* 8:4 (Winter 1959), 340.

Arkansas Steamboats

At least five steamboats carried the name *Arkansas*, including a Confederate ironclad that posed a threat to Union vessels on the Mississippi River and its tributaries during its relatively brief existence. While being constructed in Memphis, surrender of that city to federal forces in May 1862 caused the ironclad's captain to get underway and eventually reach Vicksburg, Mississippi. That August it went to the aid of Confederate forces attacking Baton Rouge, Louisiana. Engine failure later led the crew to burn the *Arkansas* on August 8, 1862.

Another *Arkansas* (1860) built for Arkansas River-New Orleans trade burned at Little Rock in September 1863. A sternwheel packet by the same name (1868) ran in Arkansas River-New Orleans trade. During December 1870 it set a record by delivering 2,301 bales of Arkansas cotton to New Orleans. New owners used this steamer in the Upper Mississippi, but ice destroyed it during 1884. (Way 29.)

An artist's rendering of the ironclad *Arkansas*. Arkansas Territorial Restoration.

Bluella: sternwheel packet (1868) built at Arkadelphia, Arkansas for Arkadelphia-Camden trade. (Way, 56.)

Blue Wing No. 2: sidewheel packet (1850) seized by a U. S. gunboat in December 1862. After arresting its crew for trading with the enemy, federal troops took the vessel to Helena, Arkansas for use by Union forces. Later in December, Confederates captured and burned the boat at Napoleon, Arkansas. (Way, 55-56.)

Bracelet: sidewheel packet (1857) moored at J. W. Jones landing near Little Rock when war broke out. This converted Confederate cottonclad burned in September 1863. (Way, 60.)

Bridge City: sternwheel packet (1854) renamed *Kate French* in November 1856. It went up in flames at Napoleon, Arkansas during November 1860. (Way, 61.)

Cambridge: Confederate forces commanded by Colonel G. E. LeMoyne took over this vessel about six miles above Des Arc, Arkansas in winter 1862. The colonel hailed the steamboat as it headed from Jacksonport, Arkansas to Memphis. LeMoyne loaded his men on board for passage to the Black River where he planned to meet supply wagons and additional troops. Within 24 hours of taking over *Cambridge* it hit a log and sank near Dudley's Dread, approximately 25 miles below Grand Glaise, Arkansas. The steamer rolled onto about 90 soldiers in the water as it went down. Although the total loss of life was unknown, 16 soldiers, five crewmen, two enslaved persons, and some passengers reportedly drowned during the incident. *S.H. Tucker* carried survivors to Pocahontas, Arkansas. (Huddleston, 51.)

Catahoula: troop transport that brought boilermakers from Memphis to St. Charles, Arkansas to repair *Mound City*. (Krivor, Final Report, Vol. I, 101.)

Catawba: sternwheel packet (1862) snagged and lost at Jacksonport, Arkansas in February 1866. (Way, 75.)

Celeste: sternwheel packet (1863) went down at DeValls Bluff, Arkansas during March 1865. (Way, 76.)

Centralia: sternwheel packet (1864) in Arkansas River-Memphis trade until destroyed during May 1868 after hitting the bank at Auburn landing on the Arkansas River. (Way, 76.)

Cherokee: freight boat (1863) struck a snag and went under in the White River during 1869. A Memphis *Daily Bulletin* on May 20, 1867, described the vessel. "The *Cherokee*, a canal boat with a stovepipe chimney and a tea kettle boiler, came in yesterday with a cargo comprising of ten bales of cotton and an empty whiskey jug. She is from one of the Arkansas Bayous. Our contemporaries were much disappointed at finding the whiskey jug empty."

Chester Ashley: sternwheel packet (1860) that Confederates stationed on the Arkansas River above Little Rock. In September 1863, Union soldiers burned the vessel. (Way, 84.)

Clermont: sternwheel packet (1863) in March 1867 headed to Memphis from the White River. It went into Zurdette chute near Helena, Arkansas, hit a snag, and "turned turtle," losing the cabin and boilers; one life lost. Another *Clermont* built in 1845 went down in the White River during December 1851; 20 persons died. (Way, 100.)

Commercial: ran aground in October 1867 about 47 miles from the mouth of the White River. After loading most of its freight into a lighter boat, crewmen restarted the steamer's engines, and the grounded boat jerked free. Unfortunately the steamboat hit a snag, which knocked a hole in its side. Fortunately for its owner, crewmen plugged the leak and pumped water out of the hull. (Huddleston, 69.)

Conestoga: After Union forces defeated Confederates at St. Charles, Arkansas in June 1862, Federals transported a Confederate Captain Fry and 29 of his men to Memphis aboard *Conestoga*.(Pearson, 16.)

Covington No. 2: Union gunboat sent to Helena, Arkansas from Memphis in July 1863 after the Confederate defeat at Helena. Federal forces burned it to prevent capture by Confederates during May 1864. (Way, 114.)

Des Arc: sidewheel packet (1862) caught fire "under somewhat mysterious circumstances" at DeValls Bluff, Arkansas in March 1864. The Memphis *Daily Bulletin* on March 26, 1864, reported the disaster. The account stated that while loading at DeValls Bluff the crew discovered a fire in the vessel's hold. As flames spread throughout the steamer its crew scuttled the boat, but despite their effort *Des Arc* "was consumed by the fire."

Diurnal: a sidewheel packet (1850). The September, 17, 1863, Memphis *Bulletin* reported that "From passengers on the *Clara Bell*, we learn that the *Diurnal* and *Pike* were sunk on the White River, about sixty miles above its mouth. There are no particulars of these last named disasters."

Eclipse: In October 1864 about 30 southern guerillas attacked this vessel near Clarendon, Arkansas. A mate on the hurricane deck quickly headed for lower decks when the shooting started. In his haste the crewman stumbled on a bell rope causing it to ring sharply. The partisans believed the ringing to be a surrender signal and rushed down the riverbank yelling, "'Come ashore, you damned Yankees! Come ashore, you damned Yankees!'" So said a reporter from the Memphis *Daily Bulletin* in its October 27, 1864, edition. Unfortunately for the would-be conquerors the boat steamed away, leaving them high and dry on the riverbank.

Economist: sternwheel packet (1868) for Arkansas River trade. One observer described the vessel as "an odd looking specimen designed to float on 8 inches of water." (Way, 140.)

Edinburgh: sternwheel packet (1865) ran from the Lower Ohio River to the Arkansas River. It sank in May 1873 approximately 40 miles below Pine Bluff, Arkansas. (Way, 141.)

Elwood: sidewheel ferry (1864) drafted into federal service for use on the St. Francis River. It was damaged on that river during fall 1864, but salvaged. *Ellwood*, a sidewheel packet built in 1860, also plied the St. Francis River and may have been one and the same with *Elwood*. (Way, 147.)

Era No. 6: sternwheel packet (1860) burned at Van Buren, Arkansas on the Arkansas River during December 1862. (Way, 154.)

Eugene: sidewheel packet (1860) in November 1862 struck the wrecked *Eliza* at Osceola, Arkansas; 15 persons died. (Way, 155.)

Fair Play: The steamer supplied Confederate forces along the Mississippi River until captured in August 1862 by a Union flotilla that included two companies of Missouri troops. The troopers included Frederic Benteen, who as a captain led soldiers during the 1876 battle of the Little Big Horn. His command survived by joining Major Marcus Reno's men holding a defensive position. Federals took *Fair Play* to Helena, Arkansas and released its crew, except for T. C. Benteen, the engineer, ardent Rebel, and disappointed father of a Yankee son.[118]

Fairy Queen: sternwheel packet (1866) lost in the Black River during July 1870. (Way, 160.)

Florence Miller No. 2: sternwheel packet (1863) seized by federal authorities and turned into a tinclad. Renamed *Little Rock* after the war, it burned at Clarendon, Arkansas in December 1867. (Way, 168.)

Florence Traber: sternwheel packet (1866) ran in Arkansas River-Memphis trade. After hitting a snag

[118]Evan S. Connell, *Son of the Morning Star, Custer and the Little Bighorn* (New York: North Point Press, 1984), 31-32. According to Connell. General George Custer's widow held Benteen responsible for what befell her husband by not riding to his rescue. She wrote that "I feel almost my husband's taking the pen away from me . . . I long for a memorial to our heroes on the battlefield of the Little Big Horn but not to single out for honor the one coward of the regiment," 47.

and going down below Little Rock in February 1868, salvagers raised the vessel. However, while traveling from Dardanelle, Arkansas to Memphis it ran into another snag and sank at Collins Shoal approximately 130 miles above Little Rock. A reporter described the boat as "badly broken and will be lost." (Way, 168.)

Frederic Notrebe: sternwheel packet (1860) burned at Van Buren, Arkansas during December 1862. (Way, 173.)

Frontier City: sternwheel packet (1860) operated in Arkansas River-Memphis trade. It went up the Arkansas River in January 1861 to recover "outfits" from two sunken vessels, *Cedar Rapids* and *A.H. Sevier*. After loading their salvage, *Frontier City* went down at the head of Smith's cutoff near the mouth of the river. (Way, 174.)

Glide No. 3: sternwheel packet (1864) operated in Arkansas River-Cincinnati trade in April 1865. During fall of that year it switched to an Arkansas River-Memphis route. The steamer sank at Madame Roubleau's plantation near Shreveport, Louisiana in November 1865. (Way, 189-190.)

Goldena: sternwheel packet (1862) wrecked in the cutoff between the Arkansas and White rivers during December 1865. (Way, 192.)

Golden State: arrived in Des Arc, Arkansas during January 1861. The boat's passengers had an exhilarating experience on the way from Memphis. Both this steamer and *Admiral* departed that city at the same time and raced down the river with flags waving and smoke streaming from their stacks. A dispute arose over the race, however. Those on board *Admiral* thought their boat won the competition. Passengers on *Golden State* disagreed. There was a race, they said, but ladies aboard *Golden State* became frightened and asked the captain to stop the contest. "The gallant Captain King yielded to the cries of the fair sex and allowed the *Admiral* to pass." (Huddleston, 47-48.)

Hesper

Acrimonious post-war politics, lawlessness, and violence led Arkansas Governor Powell Clayton to seek military arms for a state militia to restore order. After federal authorities rejected a request for assistance, the governor turned to private sources, and in September 1868 purchased rifles and ammunition. Author Orval Driggs Jr. explains what happened next. The arms reached Memphis, but steamship lines operating on the White and Arkansas rivers refused to accept the freight. Eventually owners of the steamer *Hesper* agreed, but the cargo never reached its destination. Opponents of the state administration "were watching the progress of the affair and making their own plans. When the *Hesper* was about twenty or twenty-five miles below Memphis, it was overtaken by a fast and heavy tug, the *Netty Jones*. Sixty or seventy armed and masked men aboard the pursuing craft opened fire upon the crew of the *Hesper*, and Captain Houston ran his boat ashore and escaped onto the land. The crew of fifteen men surrendered, and the masked men boarded Hesper; after throwing the arms and ammunition into the river, they cast the vessel adrift. Then they returned to their own boat, leaving word that Houston was not to return to Memphis on pain of death."[119]

Masked men destroying firearms aboard *Hesper* off the Arkansas shore. From *Illustrated home book of the world's great nations. Being a geographical historical pictorial encyclopedia.* Thomas Powell. Chicago: The Werner Company, 1893.

[119]Orvil Driggs, Jr., "Issues of the Powell Clayton Regime, 1868-1871," *Arkansas Historical Quarterly* 8:1 (Spring 1949), 21-22.

Guidon: sternwheel packet (1864) in Arkansas River-Memphis trade until snagged and lost in March 1870 at Harris's Crossing about 90 miles up the Arkansas River. (Way, 202.)

H. D. Mears: sidewheel packet (1860) entered Napoleon-Memphis trade, but Confederates burned it in September 1863 to prevent capture by Federals. (Way, 203.)

Holston: sternwheel packet (1864) went down at Luna landing in Arkansas during December 1870; passengers and crew narrowly escaped. (Way, 216.)

I Go: sternwheel packet (1861) burned in June 1864 at Arkansas Post, Arkansas. (Way, 219.)

Indiana: sidewheel packet (1864) lost near Chicot landing above Arkansas City in September 1875. The wreckage helped form Choctaw Bar. (Way, 224.)

Iron City: sternwheel packet (1864) made trips up the Arkansas River, but sank in the Red River during February 1868. (Way, 225.)

J. H. Miller: The August 31, 1864, Washington *Telegram* reported that in July, three Rebel lads captured *J. H. Miller*. It carried about 300 passengers and 13 Union soldiers. After the steamer ran aground about 18 miles below Pine Bluff, Arkansas, the three youths opened fire and demanded surrender. The boys convinced all aboard that they belonged to a Confederate company and persuaded crewmen and passengers to capitulate. When Union soldiers refused to give up, the youths boarded the steamer. Four Federals leaped overboard and swam away. Those who remained were locked in the boat's hold.

J. J. Cadot: On September 11, 1861, the Des Arc *Citizen* announced arrival of eight federal prisoners transported on this steamer. They were taken from Des Arc, Arkansas to Little Rock by land.

John D. Perry: On January 2, 1869, an edition of the *North Arkansas Times* reported that the steamer did "a flourishing business" in White River-New Orleans trade. However, that following May it caught fire while docked at DeValls Bluff, Arkansas. The hull broke into two pieces and went under. (Huddleston, 71.)

J. S. McCune: In March 1866 Captain Duffer of *J. S. McCune* invited Jacksonport, Arkansas residents to join an excursion trip to Batesville, Arkansas, and many accepted. "Following a delicious dinner, the tables were moved aside and the lively strains of music from the boat's band filled the air. Dancing continued during the entire trip with only an occasional intermission for additional treats," reported the Jacksonport *Herald* on March 31, 1866. At Batesville the captain "invited local residents to join the festivities, and a large number of the Batesville lads and lassies infused new life into the party aboard the steamer." All parties and steamers eventually come to an end, however. The boat burned near Little Island in south Arkansas during December 1867. The crew successfully evacuated all of the passengers, but a heroic steward remained aboard too long and perished. (Huddleston, 67-69.)

Kanawha Valley No. 2: sternwheel packet (1860) operated in White River-Memphis trade during spring 1861. The vessel later became a Confederate transport and burned at Island No. 10 in the Mississippi River during April 1862. (Way, 263.)

Kate Bruner: sternwheel packet (1861) destroyed on the White River after running into the wrecked *Lizzie Gill*. Crewmen stayed with the boat though many of them were ill with cholera. Way reports that "four died soon after she sank. Later two more died and their bodies were found on the wrecked boat" near St. Charles, Arkansas in September 1866. (Way, 265.)

Kenton: sternwheel packet (1860) served Union forces from 1863 until the war's end. While moored at Eastport on the Tennessee River during October 1864, Confederate gunners opened fire on the steamer from both shores. They reportedly hit the boat at least 50 times. One round destroyed a caisson in the engine room, rupturing the steam line and killing a watchman. Captain Dunlap maneuvered his boat out of range while crewmen extinguished a fire caused by the shelling. Way quotes witnesses who saw the steamer afterwards and claimed that "she was almost completely riddled by shot. Dunlap said later that the zeal displayed by his crew and himself was prompted by visions of spending the rest of the war in Libby Prison if captured." After the conflict this steamer changed owners several times until it hit a snag and sank near Helena, Arkansas in May 1870. (Way, 269.)

Lady Jackson: sternwheel packet (1860) lost on the White River during October 1863. (Way, 275.)

Legal Tender: sidewheel packet (1867) built to run from Memphis to the Arkansas and White rivers. During April 1871 it went up the White River on high water to Mittox Bay. The steamer picked up 95 bales of cotton and 180 sacks of seed, "the first time in 10 years a boat had been there." The steamer sank below Memphis in November 1871. After recovery and repair, it snagged and went down at Rowsey's Point about 40 miles below Pine Bluff in April 1876. (Way, 281.)

Lelia: packet (1863) snagged and lost on the White River during 1868. (Way, 281.)

Leni Leoti: sternwheel packet (1863). After being used in several trade routes, the vessel made Little Rock-New Orleans runs during 1869 and in May sank after snagging at McNeal's landing on the Arkansas River. The prior year, in August 1868, the boat ran the Upper Missouri River where Captain Haney forwarded a chilling letter to Pittsburgh, Pennsylvania quoted by Way. "Landing at a wood yard 45 miles above Fort Peck, I discovered the dead bodies of the proprietors, seven in number, supposed to have been killed by the Assonaboine Indians in retaliation for the murder of two of their tribe two months ago by wood-choppers in that same vicinity. The bodies of the whites killed were horribly mutilated and in a state of decomposition. I buried them as well as possible under the circumstances. The entire party came up with me this spring . . . and stopped at that point where they met their sad fate." (Way, 282.)

Lexington: During summer 1862 a Rebel sniper killed this Union vessel's chief engineer. The crew later captured a southern marksman firing at them from shore and tied him to their boat's wheelhouse in plain view. Though sniping continued, the prisoner survived. (Huddleston, 54-55.)

Liberty No. 2: sidewheel packet (1861) ran aground at Little Island on the White River in November 1869. The White River reached dangerously low levels that month, which made navigation exceptionally difficult. (Huddleston, 73.)

Linden: sternwheel packet (1860) became a U. S. tinclad in January 1863 and sank after snagging at Carson Towhead on the Arkansas River in February 1864. (Way, 287.)

Linnie Drown: sternwheel packet (1864) operated between Pine Bluff, Arkansas and Memphis until it ran into a snag and went down at Helena, Arkansas in September 1866. (Way, 287-288.)

Linton: sternwheel packet (1867) lost at the head of a cutoff between the Arkansas and White rivers. (Way, 288.)

Little Rock: sidewheel ferry (1865) sank at Pine Bluff, Arkansas in December 1872 after damaged by a snag. Another *Little Rock* (1863), a sidewheel packet that served as a U. S. tinclad during the war, burned at Clarendon, Arkansas in December 1867. An earlier vessel with that name, a sternwheel packet built in 1858, burned at Little Rock in September 1863. (Way, 289.)

Lizzie Gill: sidewheel packet (1865) lost in January 1866 at the mouth of the White River. (Way, 291.)

Lizzie Simmons: sidewheel packet (1859) converted into a Confederate gunboat named *Pontchartrain*. (Way, 291.)

Luminary: sidewheel packet (1863) in March 1867 rescued survivors from the wrecked *Clermont* at Helena, Arkansas. Unfortunately, *Luminary* hit a snag and went under at Montezuma, approximately ten miles below Helena in December 1869. (Way, 299.)

Maid of Peru: sidewheel packet (1865) sunk by *Robert E. Lee* on the Lower Mississippi River. Though salvaged, the boat went down at Helena, Arkansas in September 1867. (Way, 304.)

Market Boy: sternwheel packet (1862) lost at Helena, Arkansas in May 1866. (Way, 308.)

Mary Patterson: Confederate volunteers called the Jacksonport Guards transported an unusual prisoner during the Civil War while aboard *Mary Patterson*. A December 8, 1863, edition of *Stars and Stripes* told this story of events that occurred in May 1861. After stopping at Grand Glaise, Arkansas the Confederates learned that townsmen had a man nailed in a box for shipment to President Abraham Lincoln. The victim appeared in that village the previous week and seemed vague about which side he supported in the war. So the town's citizens held him prisoner. The Jacksonport Guards loaded the box onto this steamer and proceeded to Memphis. When offered his freedom after arrival, their prisoner refused to come out of the box, perhaps fearing that things might go from bad to worse. After five days he finally exited and "lives to fight the inhuman devils who thus maltreated him."

Mason: sidewheel packet (1863) lost on the St. Francis River in June 1870. (Way, 315.)

Maurepas: In an effort to block the White River and hinder a Union flotilla, Confederates sank vessels in the channel at St Charles, Arkansas above the river's mouth. During June 1862 they scuttled the gunboat *Maurepas* (1858) along with two transports, *Eliza G.* and *Mary Patterson* "in a line across the river." (Pearson, 15.)

Mayflower: at the end of 1868 competed with *Norman* and *Tempest* for White River-Memphis trade. (Krivor, Final Report, Vol. I, 109.)

Memphis: sternwheel packet (1863) at first named *Colossus*, then a U. S. tinclad, and finally the steamer *Memphis* in September 1865. It hit a snag and went under at Pine Bluff, Arkansas during December 1866. (Way, 319.)

Mercury: While steaming down the White River in 1867 during a storm it mistakenly entered the Arkansas River cutoff. After realizing his error, the pilot turned back, but the boat struck a snag and filled with water. Flood conditions and freezing weather made recovery difficult, and many survivors suffered from frostbite. Huddleston describes the fate of seven men who floated to safety on cotton bales, or so they thought. "While gliding down the wind-swept river, they all lodged on the same drift, which provided a momentary haven from the swirling waters. Seemingly safe, at least from immediate drowning, four of the men were killed when a tree was blown down, striking the drift on which they were lodged." About 20 persons died in the disaster along with 250 mules. (Huddleston, 68.)

Miami: sternwheel packet (1863). While above the mouth of the Arkansas River during January 1866, its boilers exploded with Union troops aboard. Reports indicated that 40 persons died. (Way, 321.)

Milton Brown: sidewheel packet (1859) in Confederate service until burned by Union troops at Donaldson's Point on the Arkansas River in July 1863. (Way, 322.)

Minnie: sternwheel packet (1865) designed for White River-St. Louis trade. In January 1866 it left Cairo en route to St. Louis, Missouri, but collided with a U. S. gunboat. *Gen. Anderson* came alongside and took off *Minnie* passengers. (Way, 324.) After raised and repaired, a May 14, 1867, *Louisville Democrat* reported that "she has a sugarloaf pilothouse on her, with the Goddess of Liberty with a dirty dress on her; ought to give the old girl a new frock." In November 1873 the boat snagged and sank at Leavenworth, Kansas.

Natchez: one of more than a dozen vessels with the same name. This sidewheel packet (1860) became a Confederate mail carrier between New Orleans and Memphis. In February 1861 the steamer carried Jefferson Davis to Montgomery, Alabama to be sworn in as president of the Confederacy. During April 1861, Confederate authorities dispatched it to the White River as a troop transport, which turned out to be the boat's last military assignment. About 25 miles above Yazoo City, Mississippi its crew torched the steamer to prevent capture by Federals. (Way, 337.)

New Moon: sidewheel packet (1860) continued to run between the White River and Memphis during the war. (Krivor, Final Report, Vol. I,14.)

Niagara: sidewheel packet (1864). In October 1865 the steamer *Post Boy* accidentally rammed this boat at the mouth of the St. Francis River. *Niagara* had on board black soldiers headed home. Crewmen cut holes in the cabin floor to rescue 30 of the troopers; death toll said to be 75. *Kate Hart* carried survivors to Memphis. (Way, 347.)

Ohio Belle: transported Confederate Colonel Patrick Cleburne's regiment to Pittman's Ferry in northern Arkansas during July 1861. At the war's outset many southerners thought the conflict would end quickly when their gentlemen warriors routed northern invaders. Thus riverboat travel during the conflict's first months provided festive opportunities for overly optimistic southerners. Cleburne's men enjoyed warm welcomes from Arkansas towns along their route, including Helena and Laconia. When the steamer reached Clarendon someone proposed a dance. Huddleston describes the festivities: "Soon the parlor of the hotel was crowded with tinkling feet keeping time to merry music until time to leave. The ladies accompanied the soldiers to the riverbank, where they waved a long farewell in the faint light of dawn." (Huddleston, 50.)

Only Chance: sidewheel packet (1865) lost at Douglas landing in Arkansas during November 1869. (Way, 356.)

Petrolia: entered White River-Memphis trade during the first six months of 1866. The light-draft vessel plied the White River "in double-quick time," reported the Des Arc *Weekly Citizen* on July 28, 1866.

Pine Bluff: The June 15, 1861, *Arkansas Gazette* reported that *Pine Bluff* made it to Little Rock from New Orleans with "300 tons of freight, including 700 rifles and 5,000 cartridges."

Platte Valley: sternwheel packet (1857) destroyed in January 1867 near the Arkansas shore after hitting the wrecked Confederate gunboat *General Jeff Thompson*. Estimates indicated 60 casualties. (Way, 374.)

Pontchartrain: Union gunboat *General Price* set this vessel on fire when Little Rock fell to Federals in 1863. (Way, 375.)

Post Boy: sidewheel packet (1859) served during the war as a federal dispatch boat for the Vicksburg fleet at three Arkansas towns—-Arkansas Post, Clarendon, and DeValls Bluff. It burned along with several other steamers at St. Louis, Missouri in September 1863. "Confederate spies were the arsonists by their own later admissions," according to Way. Another *Post Boy*, a sidewheel packet built in 1864, collided with *Niagara* at the mouth of the St. Francis River during October 1865. *Niagara* sank, and 75 persons died, but *Post Boy* survived. (Way, 376.)

Progress: sternwheel packet (1862) lost on the Arkansas River in December 1865; 20 persons died. (Way, 379.)

Queen City: originally a sidewheel ferry (1863) that became a federal gunboat. Troops commanded by Confederate General Jo Shelby attacked the boat at

A photo of the fifth *Sultana* taken on April 26, 1865, at Helena, Arkansas illustrates the severely overloaded steamer a day before the boiler explosion. Library of Congress.

The *Sultana* Tragedy

The *Sultana* tragedy occurred when the war ended and hundreds of Union soldiers boarded the steamer at Vicksburg, Mississippi for passage home. Though the boat had a capacity of 375 persons, perhaps as many as 2,400 climbed aboard. Many of the men suffered in southern prisoner of war camps throughout much of the conflict. The steamer exploded on April 27 near Marion, Arkansas, vaporizing the vessel and killing hundreds of persons on it. Author Jerry Potter shares Arthur A. Jones's description of the disaster he witnessed. "What a crash! My blood curdles while I write and words are inadequate; no tongue or writer's pen can describe it. Such hissing of steam, the crash of the different decks. As they came together with the tons of living freight, the falling of the massive smoke stacks, the death cry of strong-hearted men caught in every conceivable manner, the red-tongued flames bursting up through the mass of humanity."[120]

Estimates differ about the number of passengers and fatalities, and author Alan Huffman comments on the count. "Many people boarded without being counted, and the counting itself was questionable. By the most reliable counts, more than twenty-four hundred people were aboard. Of the more than seven hundred who initially survived the disaster, between two hundred and three hundred died in Memphis hospitals in the days after. Even allowing for a fairly wide margin of error, the accepted toll of about seventeen hundred made it the worst known maritime disaster in American history, and it would remain so even after the sinking of the *Titanic*."[121]

Sultana Explosion, *Harper's Weekly*, May 20, 1885.

---

[120]Jerry Potter, *The Sultana Tragedy: America's Greatest Maritime Disaster* (Gretna, LA: Pelican Publishing Co., 1992), 83. The magnitude of this tragedy passed largely unnoticed, due to the fact that Abraham Lincoln was assassinated that month. Most national press coverage focused on Lincoln's death and the consequences for a troubled nation.

[121]Alan Huffman, *Sultana* (New York: Harper Collins, 2009), 232. Often the steamer's horrid destruction and enormous loss of life overshadow an additional chapter in the tragedy. More than 1,800 of the men aboard were headed home after years in Confederate prison camps. At Andersonville and Cahaba they suffered from disease, starvation, and physical abuse. After this ordeal they were headed home to celebrate their survival, but it was not to be for most of them.

Clarendon, Arkansas in June 1864. A Confederate soldier named Coleman Smith wrote a detailed account of the attack. When the Confederates were "about a mile from Clarendon we came out of the woods in an open field, where we could see smoke from the chimneys of the gunboat." After positioning their cannon quietly so as not to be discovered they opened fire. "All at once, about four o'clock [in the morning] our four guns sent four shots crashing through the boat . . . almost simultaneously with our first shots the four hundred riflemen began a fullside [sic] on the boat, which was kept up until the pilot came out of his pilot house and waved a white flag." (Krivor, Final Report, Vol I, 107.) This 20-minute fight resulted in the death of one Union sailor, wounding of nine, and surrender of six officers and 20 men. Two seamen drowned while trying to escape by swimming to the opposite shore. After stripping the boat of small arms and the paymaster chest, Confederates set the steamer on fire to prevent recapture by Union troops.

R. C. Gray: sternwheel packet (1866) on the Arkansas River in April 1870 running between Little Rock and Fort Smith, Arkansas. (Way, 383.)

R. F. Sass: sternwheel packet (1855) lost about 15 miles below Memphis at Clark's Bar in the Mississippi River during May 1860; 17 persons died. (Way, 383-384.)

Red Rover: sidewheel packet (1857) acquired by Confederates in November 1861, but damaged by Union Army fire and abandoned near Island No. 10 on the Mississippi River. Seized there by Union forces, it went to St. Louis, Missouri for conversion into a hospital boat. Facilities on this steamer were exceptional for the times. It had bathrooms, a laundry, two kitchens, a 300-ton ice box, an operating room, an elevator from the main to cabin deck, sanitary stores, and a medical dispensary. The vessel's first mission involved aiding wounded personnel aboard *Mound City*, a Union steamer severely damaged by Confederate fire at the battle of St. Charles, Arkansas. *Red Rover* took injured men to Memphis and according to Way, Sister Angela, Superior of the Sisters of the Holy Cross Order, offered their services aboard *Red Rover*. "These women became the forerunner of the U. S. Navy Nurse Corps." After repairs at Mound City, Illinois, the hospital ship aided other wounded sailors, including some from an engagement with the ironclad *Arkansas*. From 1865 on, it served as a U. S. hospital ship. (Way, 389-390.)

Rodolph: sternwheel packet (1864) snagged and destroyed about 15 miles below Little Rock in December 1865. (Way, 401.)

Rowena: sidewheel packet (1864) struck a snag and sank opposite Helena, Arkansas during winter 1867. Passengers and crew were saved, but the boat lost. (Huddleston, 69.)

Sallie: sternwheel packet (1868) destroyed in 1872 after hitting a snag at Swan Lake on the Arkansas River. (Way, 415.)

Sovereign: joined *Admiral* and *Mary Patterson* in July 1861 at Fort Pillow, Tennessee about 40 miles above Memphis to pick up Confederate Colonel T. C. Hindman and his command. The vessel carried them to Pittman's Ferry on the Current River in northern Arkansas. (Huddleston, 49.)

St. Marys: sidewheel packet (1867). While moored at New Orleans in May 1867 a boiler exploded, and Way describes the ghastly consequences. It "went up through the cabin and roof, took off a smokestack, sailed up and out across the stern of the *Leonidas* into the ladies' cabin of the *Ruth*, smashing down through and demolished an elaborate chandelier. Four engineers were burned by steam, also a cabin boy and five deckhands, none seriously." The steamer later ran in Pine Bluff-Memphis trade until snagged and lost at Charlie Morris's landing in Tennessee during November 1872. (Way, 413.)

Tahlequah: sidewheel packet destroyed by Confederates at Little Rock in September 1863 to prevent capture by Federals. (Way, 443.)

Tenas: formerly *Tom Suggs*. It transported Confederate troops to the Current River until captured in August 1863 on the Little Red River by *Cricket*, a federal sternwheeler. (Krivor, Final Report, Vol. I, 103.)

35th Parallel: sidewheel packet (1859) in Arkansas River-New Orleans trade. At the start of the war Confederate authorities converted it into a cottonclad, but burned the boat during March 1863 to prevent capture by Union forces. (Way, 450.)

Trenton: sternwheel packet (1869) connected at Camden, Arkansas with *Gov. Allen* for Arkadelphia, Arkansas trade. (Way, 459.)

Tuscaroras: Confederate gunboat exploded at Harbeth's landing above Helena, Arkansas in winter 1861. (Way, 460.)

Utah: packet (1869) went from St. Louis to Fort Smith, Arkansas in March 1870 with 600 tons of freight, supposedly the largest cargo to be hauled there on a single steamer. In March 1877 it burned at an island opposite Vicksburg, Mississippi. (Way, 465.)

Van Buren: sternwheel packet (1866) hit a snag on the Arkansas River and went down above Pine Bluff, Arkansas in October 1869. During 1893, Van Buren, Arkansas builders constructed another vessel with the same name. (Way, 466.)

Victory: sternwheel packet (1864) operated in Napoleon-Memphis trade during 1869, but later turned into a towboat. (Way, 469.)

Virginia: sidewheel packet (1865). One of at least six vessels named *Virginia*, this one became "fatally snagged" at Osceola, Arkansas in October 1871. (Way, 471.)

Welcome: sidewheel packet (1863) burned at St. Louis, Missouri in July 1864. After being rebuilt and sold several times, the steamer ran in White River-New Orleans trade until destroyed by fire at New Orleans. (Way, 483.)

Up in Smoke

The war killed much steamboat traffic along Delta rivers, but peace resurrected it in glamorous form. Newspapers and journals reported the launching of many luxurious steamers during the 1870s, and Herbert Quick and Edward Quick explain the protocol. "When a boat is launched at sea a bottle of wine is spilt over her bow. Steamboatmen [sic], however, seldom spilled wine over any part of their craft. Whatever there was to drink they made use of themselves. And it was usual at the launching of a big boat for the builder to prepare a barrel of egg-nogg and set it in a convenient place, with tin cups around it, for the free disposal of the crowd. Instead of pouring a libation into the river, they poured it into themselves where they were sure it would do some good."[122]

Unfortunately during 1870 there were about as many boats destroyed as launched. The two historians describe a common cause. "Throughout all history of steamboating there is one phrase that constantly recurs: Sunk by exploding boiler. In those four words are packed the fate of so many steamboats that the list becomes a solemn, fearful litany. Of the several disasters faced by the steamboats the most sudden and terrible were those caused by the bursting of the boilers. For in that moment, for which there had been no preparation, the scalding steam enveloped the boat even as the sound of the explosion was heard; and woodwork and humanity were blown out by the terrific blast."[123] Boiler explosions "came about in many ways. A boat might be racing, trying to force her steam to pass the other boat; and the engineer, helping his utmost, would be holding down the safety valve with a rope or with extra weights." When the boat "spurted ahead, the steam pressure would be too great for the boilers; and the boat would come to a stop, shiver as if to take a plunge, and then be hidden under the cloud of hissing steam that rolled about her. Or again, the water might boil too low in the boilers and a flue, above the reduced water level, would become red-hot, weaken; and out would roar the steam, rending the casing."[124] Though causes of accidents varied, the effects could be disastrous—-people blown to bits, burned alive, or drowned in an effort to escape. Despite the frequency of boiler explosions and the horrific consequences, impediments in Arkansas rivers remained a critical danger to steamboat traffic. This fact became obvious when in 1870 a U. S. survey boat, *City of Forsyth,* completed a study of two rivers. In the Black River "there were 11,936 trees, 2,019 snags, and two wrecks. In White River from Jacksonport to DeValls Bluff there were 2,015 trees and 839 snags," reported the *Arkansas Gazette* on October 21, 1870.

---

[122]Quick and Quick, 116.

[123]Quick and Quick, 296-297.

[124]Quick and Quick, 297.

Boats Built, Destroyed, or Noteworthy: 1870

A. J. White: sidewheel packet (1870). During late November 1878 en route from Memphis to Helena, Arkansas the vessel arrived at Glendale, a railroad landing opposite Helena. It ran into a snag there and sank. (Way, 2.)

American or *America*: Four persons drowned when this sternwheel ferry sank near Little Rock during January 1870. (Tippitt, 1870, 5.)

Carrie V. Kountz: sternwheeler en route from the Ouachita River to St. Louis, Missouri in May 1870 ran aground in the chute of Island No. 95 on the Mississippi River. After breaking its hog chain the vessel entered this chute for repairs. Captains expected a boat's engineer to repair hog chains on the spot. The crew dug a pit on shore as long as the broken chain, which was placed in the hole with broken ends together. Filled with wood that the crew set on fire, the trench became a huge forge. When the chain reached a sufficient temperature an engineer sealed the broken spot. After slow cooling, the repaired chain would be installed. (Tippitt, 1870, 11, 12, 16.)

Cherokee: sternwheel packet (1870) went down during January 1873 in the Arkansas River. *T. F. Eckert* tried to raise the boat but failed. (Way, 83.)

Edinburg: sank in the Mississippi River at Island No. 49. Though raised, the vessel struck a snag in the Arkansas River during June 1870 and was a total loss. (Tippitt, 1870, 10.)

Ella Hecht: sternwheel packet (1870) constructed at Pocahontas, Arkansas. (Way, 146.)

Emma No. 3: sternwheeler collided with a snag in the chute of Island No. 35 in the Mississippi River approximately 50 miles above Memphis in February 1870. The steamer careened while sinking, upsetting stoves in the cabin which caused a fire. Officers launched a yawl and succeeded in holding back male passengers until all the females were aboard as well as the yawl crew. However, before the yawl could be cleared from the vessel, flames burst out in the cabin with such fury that other persons could not be restrained from jumping into the yawl, swamping it. All the women and many others died. Survivors reached shore by clinging to planks, cotton bales, and doors torn from cabins. About 70 persons perished in the accident. (Tippitt, 1870, 6.)

Jefferson: burned during March 1870 on the Black River; boat and cargo a total loss. (Tippitt, 1870, 9.)

J. S. Dunham: sternwheel packet (1870) operated in Arkansas River-New Orleans trade. It went down about six miles below Little Rock in April 1871 while carrying railroad rails imported from France. (Way, 237.)

Lizzie Gill: St. Louis-New Orleans packet departed Memphis in January 1870, but swamped and went down in Scrubgrass Bend above Napoleon, Arkansas. A pilot on watch ran the boat onto a sandbar where it settled. *Magenta* came to the rescue and took off 60 wet mules. (Tippitt, 1870, 3-4.)

Maggie Hays: Disaster struck this steamer (1864) in February 1870 when its boilers exploded on the Mississippi River near Helena, Arkansas. The boat loaded out at New Orleans for a trip to St. Louis, Missouri with 20 passengers, a full crew, and sugar products. Crewmen maneuvered the steamer to land, but it burned to the water line; six persons died, and the boat became a total loss. (Tippitt, 1870, 5.)

Mary Boyd: Arkansas River-Memphis packet struck the wreck of Confederate gunboat *Jeff Thompson* in the Mississippi River about four miles below Memphis in October 1870, according to one press account. *G. W. Cheek* rushed to assist along with *T. B. Allen*. A discrepancy arose as to which wreck *Mary Boyd* hit. On watch during the incident, Captain Frank Hamilton claimed that his boat struck the wrecked Confederate gunboat *Beauregard*, not *Jeff Thompson*, which supposedly went down near the Arkansas shore opposite President's Island. *Walt Allen* and *Alps* pulled *Mary Boyd* to a Memphis drydock for repairs. (Tippitt, 1870, 16-17.)

Nightingale: sternwheel packet (1863) sank in the Arkansas River during March 1870 about 50 miles above the river's mouth. The steamer started at Cincinnati, Ohio bound for Little Rock and Fort Smith, Arkansas. (Tippitt, 1870, 9.)

Robert Hardy: ferry built in 1870. According to the January 7, 1878, Pittsburgh *Gazette*, "The *Robert Hardy* built for service at Little Rock is reported to be a failure, having been badly constructed, with machinery and motive power improperly adapted to the boat."

R. P. Converse: hit a snag in June 1870 at Jacksonport, Arkansas while assisting workers building a bridge. (Tippitt, 1870, 12.)

R. P. Walt: luxurious sidewheel packet operating out of Memphis in January 1870. A January 21, 1870, Memphis *Daily Appeal* declared the boat to be "a handsome steamer constructed of the very best material and is as staunch as any steamer afloat." A *Waterways Journal* article by Donald T. Wright published on August 29, 1929, noted that on top of the steamer's pilothouse "was a bale of cotton made of some sort of metal that glittered like gold."

Ruth: sternwheel packet (1870) hauled cotton out of the White River to New Orleans. It burned on the White River during 1879. (Way, 406.)

S. C. Day: According to Tippitt, this sternwheel packet (1869) sank near Gaines Landing on the Mississippi River in 1870. (Tippitt, 1870, 15.) Way has the vessel, or one with the same name, going down at Vicksburg, Mississippi in September 1870 after being swamped due to swells generated by *City of Alton*. He reports one life lost. (Way, 407.)

Seminole: sternwheeler in March 1870 arrived at New Orleans with 360,000 pounds of pork from White River planters. (Krivor, Final Report, Vol. I, 111.)

Sioux City: sidewheel packet (1870) sank in the Arkansas River during October 1871. Salvagers pumped out the vessel, and after repairs it entered northern river trades. (Way, 428.)

W. A. Caldwell: sank in December 1870 at Caldwell's Bend in a cutoff between the White and Arkansas rivers. Rescuers saved the cotton cargo, but the boat was a total loss. (Tippitt, 1870, 18.)

Natchez, above, and *Robert E. Lee* at the time of their famous race. Way's Packet Directory.

The Great Mississippi River Steamboat Race between *Natchez* and *Robert E. Lee* inspired numerous romanticized depictions of the event, such as this Currier and Ives rendering.

The Great Steamboat Race

Perhaps the most famous race in steamboat history, and there were many of them, began on June 30, 1870. *Robert E. Lee* pulled out of New Orleans, Louisiana at seven minutes until five on a Thursday afternoon and *Natchez* five minutes later. *Lee* reached St. Louis, Missouri in three days, 18 hours, and 14 minutes. *Natchez* made it in three days, 21 hours, and 58 minutes. St. Louis luminaries honored both captains with a reception and a medal. *Lee's* success may be attributed to its skipper's craftiness. Captain John W. Cannon stripped his vessel of spars, dunnage, paying passengers, and freight. He arranged to have coal barges in midstream upriver so that he could pick up fuel while still running. As a result of the captain's shortcuts, many bettors, the losing ones of course, accused him of cheating and refused to honor their wagers. Way's compendium lists several vessels named both *Natchez* and *Robert E. Lee,* which makes their identities confusing.[125]

Steamboat races usually occurred in the spring, when business was low and rivers high. Winning a race made for good publicity, and many boats vied for bragging rights. This preoccupation with speed appears to have been endemic in 19th Century river traffic. According to Way, "The immutable stars governing the affairs of steamboat men prescribe in such case—-the laws of the United States notwithstanding—-that the engineer stop the doctor, blow down the boilers, hang grate bars on the safety valve, prod the firemen. The mate trims his boat. The captain bites his cigar and paces on the roof. The pilot skins close to the bar, hugs the point and feels for the best water. The passengers shout and jeer, cooks wave aprons, and in a flash—- by mutual consent and without the exchange of any arrangement—-two white comets soar side by side leaving to the rear horizontal columns of cumulous soot." Though many observers and sporting men encouraged racing, some newspaper editorial writers did not. One had this to say. "Boats that race should not be patronized; they are about as apt to land their passengers in eternity as in Wheeling, West Virginia or Pittsburgh, Pennsylvania."[126]

---

[125]Way, 397-398.

[126]Way, *Horns,* 55-56.

A typical Mississippi River view from the pilothouse—steamboat traffic up and down the river and a shoreline dotted with plantations. Library of Congress.

View from the Pinnacle

Way stresses that riverboat captains possessed enormous power and prestige. The author shares a letter written during the 1870s by Captain P. Miller of *Thompson Dean* to his children describing his view from the pinnacle. "We leave Memphis always on Wednesday night, every alternate week. We generally start with one or two thousand bales of cotton and fifty or sixty passengers. After stops that night to pick up additional bales we arrive Helena (90 miles) at daylight." There the vessel would spend three or four hours, sometimes longer. Following Helena, the steamer picked up additional cargo at several river locations including the White River and Napoleon, "adding 30, 50, or 100 bales of cotton and hundreds of sacks of cottonseed at each place, and passengers are getting on and off at every landing.

"The cotton bales, as you know, are about five feet long, two feet thick, and three feet wide, and weigh about 500 pounds each. The seed is in sacks nearly the size of a wheat sack and weigh about 120 pounds per sack. Friday morning we usually reach Chicot City." South of there were wealthy plantations with landings close together. They were "yet white with unpicked cotton, although the pickers have been three months at work.

"The darkies come running from the fields in droves to see 'de big *Dean*' and our brass band has an appreciative audience." Farther down the steamer stops at Arkansas City, Gaines Landing, Point Chicot, Sunnyside, and numerous points along both sides of the Mississippi River. "By this time it is Saturday night, and we begin to notice that we are entering a different country and climate.

"From Memphis to White River is an almost unbroken wilderness except at the little landings I have mentioned, but the past 24 hours we have been in a better country, and the weather is growing warmer." By Sunday morning "we are looked for by every darky and colored child along the shore for the next 100 miles. Sunday is their holiday, the day of their best clothes, and our band plays for them as we take on" more cargo. "The antics of these darkies—-old, middle aged, and young—-as they cut up on a Sunday under the influence of a brass band is more than I can hope to convey even a faint idea of, a circus wouldn't hold a candle to it.

"We are now loaded, 5,000 bales and 10,000 sacks, and the cotton is twelve tiers high on our guards. If our passengers get a peep of daylight they have to go on the hurricane deck or in the pilothouse. Our guards are dragging the water and our mates and our 100 men on deck are worn out with four days of constant work day and night." At Vicksburg, Mississippi "we take on 2,000 bushels of coal here . . . and stretch off to Natchez. We are there at daylight on Monday morning, and the flowers begin to come on board, sent by the friendly hands of those who are connected with us in a business way.

"After this we are in a different country. The cotton plantations have disappeared, and far as we can see is sugar cane, looking very much as cornfields do in summer with you. The steam from the sugar mills is seen in all directions. Liveoak, and orange, and china trees dot the landscape, and there are elegant mansions along the [river] so close to one another as to make an almost continuous village, and over all the fleecy clouds and bright sunshine of a continuous summer.

"Sometime during Tuesday afternoon the church steeples of New Orleans come into view, and we are over an hour making the circuit of the crescent on which the city is built. About 4 p.m. we move into our dock at the foot of Canal Street where a thousand or two of Negroes, French, Italian, Mexicans, etc., speaking almost every language under the sun, wait our arrival. After the last line is secure I leave the deck with a feeling of relief that another trip is ended."[127]

---

[127]Way, 453-454.

Boats Built, Destroyed, or Noteworthy: 1871

Argosy: lodged on the riverbank at Batesville, Arkansas and abandoned. (Tippitt, 1871, 14.) Way attributes the Batesville mishap to a boat named *Argos* constructed in 1864. The Pittsburgh *Commercial* on March 26, 1864, described the vessel as the "lightest draught boat of the season . . . now at the landing. She is named *Argos*." According to Way, the steamer sank at Batesville in July 1871. (Way, 28.)

Batesville: The Pittsburgh *Commercial* dated March 29, 1871, reported that the steamer *Batesville* went up the White River to Buffalo Shoals, Arkansas and brought out 475 bales of cotton at $4.50 to $5 a bale. In March 1873 the vessel ran in White River-Memphis trade. Another *Batesville* (1875) in May 1876 raced *Archie P. Green* from Batesville, Arkansas to Newport, Arkansas and reportedly won by a length or two. In October 1878 its owners advertised this *Batesville* for Helena-St. Francis River trade. (Way, 39.)

Belle of Texas: sidewheel packet (1871) purchased for Little Rock-Memphis trade. After an ownership change in January 1879 it departed New Orleans, but shifting winds blew the stacks overboard, which damaged the doctor engine. Captain Si O. Hemenway beached his boat about eight miles south of Mosquito Inlet, and he "sloshed 35 miles in water ankle to waist deep to get aid." (Way, 45.)

Celeste: sternwheel packet (1864) twisted and broken after striking a log at Salvers chute about 40 miles above Pine Bluff, Arkansas in December 1871. (Tippitt, 1871, 11.)

City of Chester: constructed in May 1871 for Memphis-St. Louis trade. It caught fire in 1877 while tied up at the Memphis elevator. Flames spread rapidly, and to save the elevator, workers cut loose the steamer, which floated downstream and lodged on a bar near Arkansas Point. Two barbers and a mail clerk died in the accident. (Tippitt, 1871, 9.)

City of Helena: This vessel (1871) possessed a combination of speed and elegance that made it an Anchor Line "brag boat." In February 1885 *Ida Darragh* tied up to an Anchor Line wharfboat in Memphis. The crew discovered a fire amid cotton on its outer guard, and the conflagration quickly spread to the wharfboat and *City of Helena*, also moored there. The blaze consumed both vessels in 15 minutes. (Tippitt, 1871, 2.)

Emma C. Elliott: sidewheel packet (1871) built for White River-New Orleans trade. (Way, 149.)

Fort Smith: Arkansas River-Memphis packet (1866) struck a snag at the mouth of the White River in October 1871 with 370 bales of cotton on board; crew saved the cotton, but lost the boat. (Tippitt, 1871, 19.)

Jennie Howell: sternwheeler (1871) used in Arkansas River- New Orleans trade. It hooked a snag near Shawneetown, Illinois in July 1873. Dispatched to rescue passengers and freight, the *T. F. Eckert* crew found people ashore "in a high state of intoxication enjoying boxes of wine floated from the wreck." *Belle Vernon* collided with the wreck about a month later and was destroyed. (Way, 245.)

Katie Morrison: small packet went down near Helena, Arkansas in March 1871 after coming from the St. Francis River with a load of cotton. The steamer filled with water and floated downriver before settling on a sandbar; a total loss. (Tippitt, 1871, 12-16.)

Petrolia No. 2: tramp packet (1864) working the White and Black rivers. It snagged and sank during February 1871 approximately 15 miles below Pocahontas, Arkansas. According to the Memphis *Avalanche* an engineer shot and killed a deck hand who he caught plundering the vessel's freight. Authorities jailed the engineer. (Tippitt, 1871, 3.)

Rhoad: St. Francis River packet operated between Helena and Marianna, Arkansas. It went under in August 1871 after sustaining snag damage; a total loss. (Tippitt, 1871, 14.)

Roseville: While going down the Arkansas River headed to New Orleans in 1871 the steamer struck a snag at Sandy Bayou Crossing roughly 20 miles above the Arkansas River's mouth. The vessel went down with about 1,000 bales of cotton on board; a total loss. (Tippitt, 1871, 12-13.) Way mentions a boat by this name built at Ozark, Arkansas in 1891. "Lost on the Arkansas River at Sandy Bayou Crossing," he says. Way mentions another *Roseville* constructed at Sparda, Arkansas in 1879. (Way, 403.)

Seminole: during February 1871 arrived at New Orleans with 1,823 bales of White River cotton transported for $3.00 per bale. (Huddleston, 77.)

S. Thayer: snagboat that worked in the White River from November 1871 to January 1872 removing 54 snags, three drift piles, and 422 trees. (Huddleston, 32.)

T. L. McGill: steamer (1862) departed Memphis in September 1871 carrying about 1,000 tons of freight and 115 people. At Shoo Fly Bar about three miles above the St. Francis River it needed to lighten up to pass over the bar. The crew put approximately 200 tons of freight on the Mississippi shore. They planned to unload a like amount of cargo on the Arkansas side and return to pick up freight deposited on the Mississippi shore. However, when crossing the bar the boat grounded. While crewmen attempted to spar-off the steamer with derricks they discovered a fire. During the intensely cold night, with gale winds and sheets of snow, an iron stove in an apartment aft of the wheelhouse set the woodwork on fire. In less than 10 minutes the blaze raged "in mad fury." The fire spread so rapidly "that there was no such thing as order. People threw cotton bales and boxes overboard and took refuge on them. Others jumped into the river." Prior to the fire *A. J. White* passed the grounded *McGill* and reached Henderson's landing to put off a passenger. When a glow on the horizon indicated distress, *White* steamed toward the burning boat joined by the steamer *St. Francis*, which had been at O.K. landing. Both vessels rushed downriver to render assistance. *Henry C. Yaegar*, about one-half mile below *McGill*, launched a lifeboat and a yawl into the river, and crews battled against a stiff current to reach the burning steamer. They saved some people, but on the second trip the yawl could not reach those clinging to the stern because of heat and flames. Upon arrival, *White* and *St. Francis* lowered their boats and saved those they could. About 57 persons survived, but 58 did not; cargo and vessel a total loss. (Tippitt, 1871, 5-6.)

Thomas H. Allen: in White River-Memphis trade during May 1871. (Way, 450.)

Yellow Hecher: packet serviced the Black and White rivers and sank during 1871 in the Black River; a total loss. (Tippitt, 1871, 11.)

Georgia Lee stuck in ice. Though difficult to believe, ice floes travelled as far south as the Lower Mississippi and crushed vessels along the way.

A Mass of Splinters

An unusual problem hampered Lower Mississippi commerce during December 1872. Intensely cold weather created ice that closed the river to commercial traffic. Huddleston describes its effect on the steamers *Chas. Bodeman, Nick Longworth, Illinois,* and other boats stuck in ice. Ice floes destroyed many vessels moored at Memphis. On December 26 and 27, "ice jammed into the steamers docked there with such force that some were reduced to a jumbled mass of splinters." Heavy chunks of ice destroyed *Belle of Pike, Helen Brooks, Laura, Summer Coon,* and *Undine* and damaged *Pat Cleburne, Andy Baum, Arlington, St. Francis, Nellie Thomas,* and *West Wind.* Moored above the dry docks, *Celeste* was carried past the city and out of sight by crunching ice flows. Ice pushed *R. P. Walt* into the bank with such force that its hull was shattered. *City of Augusta* also received damage when its starboard guard went under the larboard wheel of a twisted *R.P. Walt.*[128] The Memphis *Avalanche* on January 18, 1873, reported that "several dozen [boats] are lying huddled below Beale Street, a few being moored at Central Landing above the steamboat wharf and opposite the foot of Washington Street. Over a dozen boats are awaiting a chance to get in and for lack of room are tied up about the islands above Wolf River."

An icestorm on the White River trapped *Quapaw* near DeValls Bluff. Prairie County Historical Museum.

---

[128] Huddleston, 80-81.

The *Glasgow* Saga

Glasgow, a packet built in 1872, entered White River trade. In October of that year Captain Abner Bird took the steamer upriver from Memphis to escape the clutches of a sheriff, leaving his crew and creditors in the lurch for about $1,500. Deputy U. S. Marshal Atlee on *Grand Tower* gave chase. The *Glasgow* pilot, Si Dougherty followed on *Julia*. Captain Bird had earned an unsavory reputation, according to press accounts. While master of *Republic,* a dozen years prior to the *Glasgow* caper, he acquired notoriety by sliding quietly out of New Orleans with a couple of sleepy sheriffs and a "bacchanalianly" [sic] disposed marshal on board, each of whom he set ashore in a dark cypress brake somewhere below Baton Rouge, Louisiana. A year or two later Bird added to his negative reputation by entangling sundry persons in financial embarrassment with *Admiral* and *Sovereign,* both of which he commanded at that time. The captain acquired additional fame by getting *John D. Perry* into hock and having to sell it to compensate creditors.

After gaining control of *Glasgow*, which he operated for a trip or two from the White River to Louisville, Kentucky, Bird laid up during the summer at Jacksonport, Arkansas. When he arrived in Memphis the captain (spelled Baird in some sources) found that he lacked $1,500 to settle with *Glasgow* crewmen and pay for provisions. Several members of the boat's deck crew sued for their wages so Bird borrowed enough from Old Si, his pilot, to pay them off. The captain then pawned his watch for six dollars and invited the boys to a theatre, including Old Si, Windy Jack, the mate, and several others. They naturally wondered at "Bird's sudden generosity and plethoric [sic] wallet," according to Tippitt, and their wonder increased when after the theatrical performance their captain treated them to cigars and drinks all around and paid cash for the same. About 2 a.m., when the boys went to the foot of Washington Street where they supposed their boat to be, there was no *Glasgow*. The steamer departed quietly after a trusting Captain Selby purchased one-half interest in the vessel. When *Belle Memphis* arrived from St. Louis, Missouri its crew reported passing *Glasgow* "running like a scared hound" and *Grand Tower* in hot pursuit. Authorities seized *Glasgow* at New Madrid, Missouri and sold the steamer at Cairo, Illinois. (Tippitt, 1872, 16.)

Was the *Glasgow* saga finished? Hardly. W. D. Holcomb bought the steamer in 1873 at a marshal's sale on the recommendation of Captain Young, a supposedly astute river man. The plan called for putting the boat in White River-Memphis trade, and the financial projections looked like this: 1,000 bales of cotton at $2.50 per bale each run, making four trips per month. This scenario would earn the owner $10,000 one way each month. If the steamer only brought in one-half that amount on its return, total income would be $15,000 per month. Deduct $3,000 for expenses, and the vessel would net a handsome profit of $12,000 per month. If the boat only cleared half that much per month, it still would be a good return on investment. Unfortunately for Holcomb, the plan did not work out that way. On its first round trip from Memphis to the White and Black rivers, receipts amounted to only $350. *Glasgow* ran aground and had to pay the steamer *Legal Tender* $200 to pull it off a bar. The boat knocked down a chimney in the Black River, and at the end of the trip came out $5,000 short. Thus did Holcomb learn an expensive lesson about the vagaries of steamboat investments. (Tippitt 1873, 14.)

Boats Built, Destroyed, or Noteworthy: 1872

Ashland: sternwheel packet (1872) ran in Little Rock-New Orleans trade. During March 1878 it struck a bank on the Red River. *Susie Silver* assisted for twelve hours and claimed salvage rights, collecting $5,000. (Way, 31-32.)

Cherokee: Among at least nine vessels that shared this name, it went under in the Arkansas River during January 1872 while bound for Little Rock. (Tippitt, 1872, 17, 20.)

Clara L: constructed at Pocahontas, Arkansas during 1872. (Way, 99.)

De Smet: sidewheel packet (1872) locked in ice at Helena, Arkansas that winter. This incident became one of many difficulties faced by Joseph LaBarge, the steamer's captain and owner. Way says that during the captain's trip to Fort Benton, Montana "he was arrested for selling alcohol to the Indians," but cleared of the charge. After the boat changed hands several times it burned in June 1886 near Newport, Arkansas. (Way, 125-126.)

Exporter: built in 1872 for Arkansas River-New Orleans trade. On March 16, 1872, the steamer set a record for the most freight hauled out of the Arkansas River. In April 1875 it burned at New Orleans. (Tippitt, 1872, 1, 15.)

George C. Wolff: constructed in 1872. While at St. Francis Island above Helena, Arkansas in August 1873 its boilers blew up killing 12 and wounding 15 crewmen. (Tippitt, 1872, 13, 21.)

Great Republic: According to a Memphis *Avalanche* from January 14, 1872, the vessel passed by "flying light" from New Orleans to Cairo, Illinois to pick up the Russian Grand Duke Alexis and his entourage. However, frozen sections of the river caused the royal party to take a train to Memphis. On February 2 the Duke and companions arrived at Memphis on a special train. Since *Great Republic* did not travel south due to ice on the upper river, on February 7 the steamer *James Howard* transported the royal party and about 30 guests to New Orleans for $10,000. Though a popular steamer, *Great Republic* failed as a commercial carrier. The boat changed hands several times, usually to the financial detriment of new owners, and after major structural modifications in March 1876 was renamed *Grand Republic.*

Importer: owners fitted out the steamer (1866) with cotton guards designed to increase cargo capacity. Loaded with 2,000 bales for New Orleans, it sank in March 1872 at Horsehead, roughly 140 miles above Little Rock. The boat proved to be a total loss, but salvagers saved some of the cargo and machinery. (Tippitt, 1872, 3, 6, 16.)

John B. Maude: steamer (1872) ran in Memphis-New Orleans trade. In January 1875 it went down at O. K. landing about 40 miles above Helena, Arkansas on the Mississippi River while bound south with 800 bales of cotton. (Tippitt, 1872, 1, 13.)

John Means: towboat exploded at Plum Point near Osceola, Arkansas in 1872 while heading north towing empties; five persons died. (Tippitt, 1872, 15.)

John Overton: transfer steamer (1872) operating in conjunction with a Little Rock Railroad landing at Hopefield Point, Arkansas. (Tippitt, 1872, 19.) By 1872, rail competition for hauling freight had gathered momentum in Arkansas. In previous years, according to the January 14, 1871, *Weekly Herald,* an enormous amount "of state aid had been awarded to the various railroads." By the end of his term in 1871, Governor Powell Clayton "was able to report to the legislature that a number of railroads were under construction in the state; and he pointed out that almost 200 miles of track had already been laid, and that many more miles of trackage [sic] were virtually finished." However, trains running some routes moved so slow over lowlands that one wag claimed you could travel faster on foot.

Katie: An observer called this vessel (1871) "hard to hold, quite fast, and [one which] buried her head under full headway." During November 1872 it crashed into the wrecked *Holcomb* and went down at Trotter's Point below Helena, Arkansas. The *T. F. Eckert* crew hoped to raise *Katie,* but the wreck floated downriver and lodged on a bar. (Tippitt, 1872, 12, 16.)

Mary E. Poe: sternwheel packet (1872) caught fire during October 1872 approximately ten miles above Osceola, Arkansas at Daniel's Point. Flames gained such headway that the captain ran it onto a bar, forcing 65 passengers and crewmen to swim for their lives; several fatalities occurred. *City of Helena* raced to the scene, picked up stranded passengers, and took them to Memphis. The wrecked steamer came to rest in an old chute at O'Donnell Bend west of islands No. 26 and No. 27 in the Mississippi River. When *T. F. Eckert* arrived at the site on October 28 its crew found the wreck held by pirates who had driven watchmen ashore. Thieves used about 20 skiffs to carry off freight, but *Eckert* personnel saved the remaining cargo. (Tippitt, 1872, 17, 22.)

North Missouri: transfer boat (1865) held two locomotives and several railroad cars when it hit a snag in the White River during May 1872. The steamer went down approximately 14 miles above Augusta, Arkansas; boat a total loss. (Huddleston, 79.)

Thomas H. Allen: en route from Little Rock to Memphis in 1872 ran into a snag about five miles above DeValls Bluff, Arkansas on the White River. The obstruction penetrated its hull and tore out a starboard guard. Water rose to the hurricane roof. (Huddleston, 79-80.)

Caught Between Political Factions

The steamer *Hallie* under fire. Arkansas History Commission.

An Arkansas steamer became a casualty in a political contest that led to violent confrontation between two state factions. Several events contributed to the dispute between rivals Joseph Brooks and Elisha Baxter, but the most contentious occurred when they faced off in a race for governor. Michael Dougan explains what happened in this convoluted contest. "Election day, November 5, 1872, reflected rather poorly on the democratic process. No returns at all came from four counties, and fraud, violence, intimidation, and multiple voting were the order of the day." Baxter allegedly won by almost 3,000 votes, "but fanatical Brooks supporters refused to accept the results." Brooks applied to the state legislature for relief and a reversal of fortune, but his appeal failed. The situation became even more complicated when a circuit court judge ruled in favor of Brooks with respect to the disputed election and swore him in as governor. "Thus on April 15, while Baxter sat in his office at the State House, Brooks supported by what Baxter called an armed force of a dozen or twenty, gave him the alternative of forcible and unseemly objection, or of such arrest and punishment as he might see fit to inflict." Baxter decided to leave, and in April 1874 the "Brooks-Baxter War" began.

Both men formed militias, and violent confrontations occurred throughout the state. "Overall, some 200 persons were killed in scattered disturbances, including some innocent bystanders in Little Rock caught between the lines when gunfire erupted."[129] When Baxter forces found out in May 1874 that a barge carrying arms and recruits to support Brooks was coming up the Arkansas River to Little Rock, about two dozen of them decided to intervene. They commandeered *Hallie* in Little Rock and set out to meet the barge. To further incite violence, about 200 Brooks supporters arrived by train at Palarm station near the riverbank and waited to ambush *Hallie*. Gunfire disabled the boat, and it drifted downstream and lodged on the southwest shore. The steamer's captain, a pilot, at least one rifleman, and several others were wounded in the exchange. The Brooks militia suffered casualties as well. Eventually, Baxter became the undisputed governor when President U. S. Grant interceded.[130]

---

[129]Dougan, 258-259; 262.

[130]Dougan, Ibid.

Napoleon: Swallowed by the River

Napoleon was founded about 1833 and became one of Arkansas's busiest trade ports with a population varying from 800 to 5,000, depending on the season and number of vessels tied up at piers. Napoleon had banks, hotels, churches, a courthouse, jail, a newspaper, theater, fire department, cotton factors, and a marine hospital. However, in 1862 a high river carried away the hospital and later came back for the entire town. According to author Elmo Howell, Mark Twain's "notes as well as internal evidence" indicate that Bricksville from *Huckleberry Finn* "was patterned after Napoleon, Arkansas." Howell describes Twain's view of the town, and it is not a flattering one. Its streets of mud were "as black as tar, and nigh about a foot deep in some places; and two or three inches deep in all the places." Twain tells of hogs "rooting and taking their pleasure in the middle of the streets until chased off by dogs sicced on them by town loafers, looking for a little excitement." Deadbeats sat on empty boxes in front of stores, "gaping and yawning, and stretching," seeking entertainment in such ways as tying a bucket to a dog's tail until the poor creature ran himself to death.[131]

Despite Twain's derogatory views about the village, the marine hospital there put the town in league with cities such as St. Louis, Missouri and New Orleans. Virtually all river laborers lacked the money to pay for medical treatment, and the result caused much misery and many deaths. As a result, in 1830 marine hospital service was extended to western rivers. "Eager for the benefits of federal expenditures, the leading river communities clamored for the erection of marine hospitals to replace the contract system for providing relief through local hospitals, physicians, and boardinghouse keepers." In 1837 the U. S. Congress provided funding for erection and operation of federal marine hospitals at key points on western rivers. Napoleon became the site of one. Hunter says that "The system of medical relief and hospitalization thus established unquestionably did much to alleviate the suffering of steamboat laborers."[132]

Napoleon, Arkansas under water ca. 1870. Arkansas History Commission.

---

[131]Elmo Howell, "Mark Twain's Arkansas," *Arkansas Historical Quarterly* 29:3 (Autumn 1970), 198.

[132]Hunter, 463.

A Daunting Task

Much praise is heaped on riverboat pilots and deservedly so. Experience gained through on-the-job training as apprentices prepared them for this daunting task, but a former pilot, Bill Heckman, added a counterclaim mentioned by author Jane Curry. "A river pilot is born, not made, and if he does not have that sixth sense, he had better plow corn."[133] How men avoided the cornfield varied. Many underwent similar initiations and training on their steps to the pilothouse, with some exceptions, Mark Twain being one. He did not arrive via the path of most pilots. Twain never worked as a deckhand, but started as a "steerman, a cub, in consideration of the sum of five hundred dollars to be paid to his mentor out of future wages. While it was common for some captains even in the early twentieth century to extract percentages or flat fees from steersmen in return for tutelage, most pilots began their careers as deckhands or members of the galley crew or clerks, and eventually worked their way up to the wheelhouse." DeVoto summarizes Twain's description of what a pilot had to know. "When I had learned the name and position of every visible feature of the river, when I had so mastered its shape that I could shut my eyes and trace it from St. Louis to New Orleans, when I had learned to read the face of the water as one would cull the news from the morning paper, and finally when I had trained my dull memory to treasure up an endless array of soundings and crossing marks, and keep fast hold of them, I judged that my education was complete."[134] Despite often humble beginnings, when trainees reached the pilothouse they became riverboat royalty, often in the service of King Cotton.

This engraving of the *Great Republic* pilothouse appeared in an October 1874 edition of *Scribner's Monthly*. In it a vigilant pilot steers the vessel amid speaking tubes to the boiler room, bell pulls, and a globe on the jackstaff to help him align the boat with a distant horizon.

---

[133]Jane Curry, *The River's in My Blood. Riverboat Pilots Tell Their Stories* (Lincoln: University of Nebraska Press, 1983), 21. The author collected stories from more than 50 pilots who worked on western rivers. Using their accounts she discusses the traditions, initiations, and training of these critical officers who guided steamers from departure to arrival.

[134]Bernard DeVoto, editor, *The Portable Mark Twain,* From *Old Times on the Mississippi* (New York: Viking Press, 1968), 89-93. Though this volume provides a diverse sampling of Twain's literary output, DeVoto includes a lengthy excerpt from *Old Times On The Mississippi.*

Helena: Shelter Against the Law

A drawing of Helena, Arkansas from the September 16, 1871, edition of *Every Saturday*.

Helena became a prominent Mississippi River town that Sylvanus Phillips helped establish, naming it Helena after his daughter. Worley quotes a May 1837 ordinance that "designated the river front of the town as reaching from the southeast corner of York Street to the elm tree, opposite the store of Bowie and Hornor. This front was for the exclusive use of steamboats in loading and unloading provided that no steamboat lie at the landing more than three days at a time. The space above the steamboat landing was reserved for keelboats and flatboats, but they must not tie up above the large cottonwood tree." These vessels also used an area "from the elm tree as far down as the corporation extends." Livestock haulers had to depart when ordered by the wharf master or face a $30 fine.[135]

Travel down streets crowded with rivermen could be a walk on the wild side, but one that DeVoto describes as quintessentially American. The author believes that the steamboat age "perfectly expressed America. Even the debris through which the age passed was vital and eloquent—-the dens at Helena and Natchez and all the waterside slums; the shanty boats with their drifting loafers; the boats of medicine shows . . . minstrel troupes, doctors, thugs, prophets, saloon keepers, whoremasters."[136] Salacious reputations of river towns spread through anecdotes and tall tales. Featherstonhaugh heard about Helena from an acquaintance who described its inhabitants as "counterfeiters, horse stealers, murderers, and sich [sic] like took shelter again [sic] the law."[137]

---

[135]Worley, 2

[136]Devoto, *Twain's America*,106.

[137]Featherstonhaugh, II, 9.

Boats Built, Destroyed, or Noteworthy: 1873

Fannie Tatum: built in 1873 for Arkansas River-St. Louis trade. It sank in the Mississippi River near Fort Chartres, Missouri approximately 50 miles below St Louis, Missouri in September 1880 while taking on cargo. (Way, 161.)

J. F. Joy: sidewheel transfer boat (1873) sent from Nebraska to Helena, Arkansas in the late 1880s. The vessel went under at Helena in January 1895. (Way, 230.)

Josie: combination packet and towboat (1873). While being towed from the White River to St. Louis, Missouri it collided with *L. E. Patton* at Peter's Towhead on the Mississippi River below Memphis and went down. (Tippitt, 1873, 5.)

Katydid: sidewheel packet (1873) placed in White River-Vicksburg trade. (Way, 268.)

Legal Tender: During April 1873, two passengers heading from Memphis to DeValls Bluff, Arkansas aboard *Legal Tender* became victims of a confidence game. While on board the men purchased railroad tickets from DeValls Bluff to Little Rock, or thought they did. When the two attempted to board the train they found out that their tickets were fake. The *Arkansas Gazette* warned river travelers to be "wary of this latest deception." (Huddleston, 82.)

Pink Varble: Arkansas River sternwheel packet (1865) named for a well-known riverboat captain. It snagged and sank above Auburn, Arkansas in April 1873. The cargo washed overboard when the steamer went down, and river pirates gathered it up; a total loss. (Tippitt, 1873, 10; Way, 372.)

Queen: built at Van Buren, Arkansas in 1873. (Way, 498.)

S. Thayer: In February 1873, salvagers removed machinery from this wrecked snagboat at the mouth of the White River. (Tippitt, 1873, 11.)

Passengers passing the time with a game of cards aboard *Lula Prince*. Photograph by Norman Studio. Louisiana State University Libraries, Special Collections. Thomas H. and Joan W. Gandy Photograph Collection.

Bestial Feeding

Meals aboard luxurious riverboats could be sumptuous and formal. Charles Latrobe went by steamer from the Arkansas River to Wheeling, West Virginia and with a somewhat idiosyncratic vocabulary describes dining protocol. After servers filled the table with dishes inspected by the steward, he or his assistant went to the ladies' cabin and announced the meal. This announcement "is generally followed by their appearance. They take their places at the upper end of the table, and then, and not till then, the bell gives notice that individuals of the rougher sex may seat themselves. There is little or no conversation, excepting of the monosyllabic and ejaculatory kind which is absolutely necessary." With conversation limited to monosyllabic ejaculatory requests such as pass the salt, the meal became "an uneasy ten minutes, in which the necessary act of eating is certainly stript [sic] of all the graces under which supercultivation contrives to shroud its sensuality, and is reduced to the plain homely realities of bestial feeding. Many of the males will leave the table the moment they are satisfied—- the ladies leave it as soon as they well can; and then in come the barkeepers, engineers, carpenter, pilot, and inferior officers." The third feeding is for the "coloured [sic] servants of both sexes." In between formal meals "you may lounge in the anti-chamber [sic] and watch the progress of stimulating at the bar." Many boat owners outsourced their bar operations. Entrepreneurs would bid for the right to sell liquor to passengers who needed "stimulating."[138]

Tippitt provides an 1874 menu from *Ed. Richardson,* a Memphis, New Orleans packet, which indicates the magnificent fare offered to cabin passengers:

Entrees: broiled redfish as maitre d'hotel, broiled leg mutton with caper sauce, corned beef and cabbage, chicken, Fulton Market-bred ham, and roast loin of beef, pork, turkey, and saddle of mutton.

Vegetables: mashed potatoes, rice, cabbage, hominy, turnips, and snap beans.

Condiments and miscellaneous items: gherkins, Cross & Blackwell's pickles, tomato catsup, currant jelly, piccalilli, walnut sauce, Lee & Perrin sauces, English onions, Naunsel white Spanish olives, horseradish, lettuce, cheese, chow-chow, mushroom catsup, cole slaw, John Bull's sauce, and French mustard.

Other entrees: calves feet a la Pauceline, filets of chicken with truffles, pieds de veau a la Pauceline, braised brisket of lamb with green peas, filet de poulets aux truffles, pol rine d'afneau au brasier, and avec pots vertis.

Cold dishes: corned beef, tongue, ham, and salad.

Desserts: white raisin a la Windsor pudding with vanilla sauce, lemon pie, green apple pie, petite puit d'amour, fachenneties a la fleur de orange, pound cake, lady fingers, fruit, jelly cake, and coconut praline.

Creams, jellies, fruit, and nuts: jelly de macadonia, maraschino jelly, meringue aux peche, cream a la Ronan, pecans, pineapples, figs, almonds, Brazilian nuts, raisins, English walnuts, filberts, oranges, bananas, fresh dates, and apples.

Breakfast at 7 to 9 a.m. Lunch at 1 p.m. Dinner at 6 p.m.[139]

---

[138]Charles Joseph Latrobe, *The Rambler in North America,* Vol. 1 (London: Seeley and Burnside, 1833), 292-293; 295-296. Published in two volumes, Latrobe chronicles his departure from Europe and his journey throughout the United States during 1832 and 1833, including extensive steamboat travel on the Mississippi and Ohio rivers.

[139]Tippitt, 1874, 13.

Boats Built, Destroyed, or Noteworthy: 1874

Batesville: On October 1, 1874, the *Arkansas Gazette* reported that during the previous day Jacksonport, Arkansas residents were visited by A. H. Garland, a candidate for governor. *Batesville* carried Garland and his entourage from Jacksonport to Newport, Arkansas. Passengers included Jacksonport's "fairest sons and daughters," and all received a "hearty welcome."

Crescent City: While towing five barges in 1874 its boilers exploded about eight miles below Helena, Arkansas en route from New Orleans to St. Louis. Fire destroyed the steamer's barges and about 1,300 tons of freight. Eight members of the crew died in addition to the wife of a pilot. The steamer *Phil Allin* arrived on scene soon after the explosion and rescued survivors. Running along the Arkansas shore when the explosion occurred, the boat settled on Montezuma Bar in the Mississippi River. (Unidentified newspaper report.)

Maumelle: Arkansas River packet built in 1874 for service at Memphis and on the Arkansas River. (Way, 316.)

Octavia: snagboat cleared 51 snags, one drift pile, and 1,592 trees out of the White River, according to a 1874-1875 engineer report. (Krivor, Final Report, Vol. I, 131.)

St. Francis Trader: built at Madison, Arkansas in 1874. (Way, 410.)

The year 1874 proved to be a difficult one for many port towns competing with railroad destinations. That year the Memphis and Arkansas River Packet Company abandoned its White River line. The Elliot line continued service on the river with three steamboats making regular trips—-*City of Augusta, Bannock City*, and *Legal Tender*. In addition to ever-increasing competition from railroads, riverboats were hit with a government tax that became unpopular with owners. Captain Milt Harry addressed a convention of steamboat captains that year with a speech carried by the Memphis *Public Ledger*. He complained of boats having to carry "freights at cheap rates, heavy insurance, and the bare faced cussedness of the newfangled government tax tacked on to the poor steamboatmen [sic] who can't afford to pay lobbyists to represent them in Congress."[140] Harry had strong and long connections to the Delta, where he operated for many years on the White and Mississippi rivers as a boat captain and owner.

[140]Pearson, 21.

Separate and Unequal

Black steamboat passengers experienced many of the tensions and difficulties they faced during everyday life in the post-Civil War South. In most ways they were separated from whites and not treated as equals. According to the Memphis *Avalanche* on May 24, 1875, "senators Ross and Gray, the colored councilors of Washington County, Mississippi, have sued the steamer *Illinois* because the clerk declined to provide them with their choice of staterooms and seats at the table. The case will be transferred to Jackson, Mississippi as several similar efforts have been made by black people to worry [sic] something out of the boats, hotels, and other public conveyances on this Civil Rights question." Boat owners won the lawsuit. No surprise there. Black plaintiffs in a trial held at Jackson, Mississippi during that era had little or no chance of success. Tippitt reports several Civil Rights disputes aboard steamers including this one. "A short time ago a Negro woman went on aboard the Anchor Line steamer *Capitol City* and demanded cabin passage. The clerk assigned her to a stateroom especially provided for colored passengers, but the aristocratic colored lady insisted upon being stowed away among the white people. Upon refusal of the clerk to her demands, she caused him to be arrested under the Civil Rights provision. The trial was held a few days ago before the U. S. Commissioner W. H. Bolton." He ruled that "the law had not been violated and that the officers of the steamboat had a perfect right to dispose of and locate their passengers as they thought best. This decision will probably save our steamboats a deal of unnecessary trouble."[141]

Such efforts to integrate riverboat transportation began soon after the war ended. In one instance Captain W. J. Ashford, commander of *Natoma*, found himself in legal jeopardy during July 1869. Passengers boarding his vessel at Little Rock included a Reverend White and his wife. The July 27, 1869, *Arkansas Gazette* reported that "Reverend White was a black member of the Arkansas legislature from Helena. Upon boarding, Reverend White asked for a berth for his wife in the ladies' cabin, but his request was refused. The representative was told that there was a place below for colored ladies of distinction, but that no Negro on earth could have a room in the cabin of the *Natoma*" while Ashford commanded the steamer. "Reverend White replied that he had helped to pass the public carrier law in the legislature especially for the benefit of Captain Ashford, since the captain had refused White cabin passage in 1865."[142] White sued Ashford for $10,000.

Despite many difficulties, the reverend continued his crusade. A January 21, 1870, *Arkansas Gazette* announced that White filed suit for $5,000 "against the *Liberty No. 2* because he was forced to eat in the pantry instead of at the table with white passengers." The reporter concluded that the reverend may have been entitled to damages based on Act 15, but the confrontation would "undoubtedly cause trouble." The newspaper got that part right. Continued confrontations did cause trouble. Discrimination in accommodations for black passengers aboard steamboats eventually led to this ruling from a federal judge in Pittsburgh, Pennsylvania announced in the May 28, 1878, *Arkansas Gazette*. The judge declared that "colored" passengers on steamboats were "entitled to the same treatment as white people." However, they did not have the right to eat at the same table or sleep in the same stateroom if the vessel offered facilities equal in value to those provided for white people. The judge ruled that boat captains had the right to manage their boats as they thought best. Equal treatment, wrote the gullible reporter, would ensure that "all trouble and dissatisfaction could be avoided [as the] duty of each party is set forth." A Birmingham, Alabama resident may have revealed a critical consideration in transportation disputes. "It is not important which [space] is given to the nigger. The main point is that he must sit where he is told."[143]

---

[141]Tippitt, 1875, 12.

[142]In 1868 Arkansas Governor Powell Clayton signed Act 15 into law, prohibiting racial discrimination on public carriers, steamships, railroads, streetcars and stagecoaches, along with other public areas. If convicted, punishment was not less than $200 and no more than $5,000, plus possible jail time. The law was rarely tested, however, as it was known that most all-white juries would not convict other whites.

[143]Leon F. Litwack, *Trouble in Mind. Black Southerners in the Age of Jim Crow* (New York: Alfred A. Knopf, 1998), 232. Litwack provides an account of life in the Jim Crow South, drawing on contemporary documents and first-person narratives from both blacks and whites.

Boats Built, Destroyed or Noteworthy: 1875

Arkansas City: sternwheel packet (1875) built at Arkansas City, Arkansas and originally based at Memphis. (Way, 30.)

Belle St. Louis: Four days out of St. Louis headed to Vicksburg, Mississippi the steamer (1875) sank during November 1879 close to Island No. 40 on the Mississippi River approximately 20 miles above Memphis. The Memphis *Daily Appeal* on November 15 gave a detailed account of the disaster. "Pilot Joe Carroll was at the wheel at the time of the accident. He came down to the city last night in a yawl bringing intelligence of the disaster. He stated that the *Belle* was turning cautiously by the lead at the time, the last call being 15 feet. He saw no surface indications of obstructions, no ripples or break in the water, and had no warning of presence of danger. As soon as she struck, the violence of the shock admonished [sic] him that the boat had been seriously injured, and he immediately headed her for the nearest shore, which was the Arkansas bank of the river. She made the point aimed at but soon settled in a bad place, her outside guards being in 12 feet of water. She settled in such position as to soon become badly broken up, and there are doubts about her ever being raised." The steamer carried about 20 passengers, nearly all headed to Memphis, but no injuries or deaths occurred. The point at which the boat "met her fate is about two or three miles above where the *Katie P. Kountz* of the Kountz Line was sunk in a similar manner several weeks ago. In fact . . . Island 40 has become the worst place on the river from St. Louis down in as much as the channel there has become a network with hidden obstructions such as have wrought the fate of the *Kountz* and the *Belle St. Louis*."

Ben Wood: boiler exploded in August 1875 at Dardanelle Landing on the Arkansas River. (Tippitt, 1875, 1.)

Cora Belle: burned in February 1875 at Pocahontas, Arkansas while loaded with cotton. Sparks from its stacks apparently caused the fire. Boats on Arkansas rivers carried a large volume of cotton that year. The Memphis *Avalanche* reported on July 4, 1875, that 20 vessels worked the White and Arkansas rivers between the previous September and end of June. They re-shipped from the Arkansas River 15,750 bales during that period. The sum included 2,123 bales to Memphis; 445 to St. Louis, Missouri, and the balance to other destinations. This did not account for cotton carried out of the Arkansas River by New Orleans and Vicksburg, Mississippi steamers, or others that did not normally operate on the Mississippi River. (Tippitt, 1875, 14-15.)

Creole: built at Helena, Arkansas in 1875. (Way, 496.)

Eliza Fox: small packet sprung a leak and went under in the White River during 1875. (Tippitt, 1875, 15.)

Ella: struck a log during March 1875 while en route from Memphis to Jacksonport, Arkansas. The obstacle fouled its rudder and caused the steamer to run into timber, which tore away the upper works and pierced its hull. The boat rapidly filled with water and went under; a total loss. (Tippitt, 1875, 16.)

Fort Gibson: Arkansas River packet worked between Memphis and Pine Bluff, Arkansas until the end of December 1975. It ran upon a stump and sank at South Bend in the Arkansas River. (Tippitt, 1875, 5.)

Freddie: sternwheel freighter (1875). A U. S. marshal sold this vessel in Cairo, Illinois during August 1876 for $75. "The little two dollar and six-bitt steamer *Freddie* passed here Friday on her way from Cairo to White River. A circus agent was watching for her to offer the owner a bid on her purchase, but the dinky didn't land," reported the October 20, 1876, Memphis *Avalanche*.

Kentucky: In August 1875 this multi-purpose towboat headed for the St. Francis River, hauling two barges of cabbage, kraut, potatoes, and sundries. (Tippitt, 1875, 6.)

Osceola Belle: Built in 1875 for Osceola-Memphis trade, Way says the sidewheel packet "went out in the timber above Vicksburg, Mississippi on a falling river in early 1876 and was stranded good and proper. A rise came along and *Quickstep* and *West Wind* went to the scene with two empty barges, partly filled them with water, placed them under the stranded boat's guards, and pumped them out. In such manner she was jerked back afloat." The steamer burned at a Memphis wharf in 1880. (Way, 359.)

Rene Macready: sidewheel packet (1875) ran a St. Francis River-Memphis route. During 1882 it shuttled between Memphis and Marion, Arkansas making connections with the Memphis & Little Rock Railroad. (Way, 391.)

Thomas B. Florence: snagboat (1875) used in the Ouachita and Red rivers until converted into a packet running from Rosedale, Arkansas up the White River. (Tippitt, 1875, 9.)

This *Harper's Weekly* illustration from May 26, 1866 depicts Big Rock, above, and Little Rock, below.
Big Rock referred to a bluff on the Arkansas River above what is now North Little Rock, Arkansas.
It was about two miles upriver from a smaller bluff on the opposite bank known as Little Rock.

Queen of the Mississippi Burns

Mary Bell, known as the Queen of the Mississippi, was launched in July, 1875. Builders designed steamers such as this expressly for cotton trade in southern regions, with no boiler deck guards over the main deck forward of the wheelhouse. The boiler deck did not extend beyond the hull, so cotton could be stacked tier on tier often as high as the hurricane roof. Many of these boats worked from Chicot City, Arkansas to New Orleans hauling cotton during fall and winter months. In the early 1870s, boats constructed for the lower river were sidewheelers limited to a capacity of about 5,000 bales. In the later part of the decade, when owners faced rising costs and strong competition from railroads, they turned to more economical sternwheelers.

A reporter commented about the enormous size of *Mary Bell* in a July 13, 1875, Metropolis *Times* article. "The extreme length of Captain J. Frank Hick's new boat is 325 feet; breadth 56 feet with floors 50 feet; depth of hold 11 feet; and add to this a sheer of six feet down amidship fore and aft, and a guard 18 feet wide all around, then some idea of the proportions of this gigantic vessel may be formed." According to the St. Louis *Times* on September 17, 1875, "a large number of boatmen examined this mammoth craft yesterday, and all pronounced her a 'big thing.'" An October 17 St. Louis *Times* edition crowned *Mary Bell* "Queen of the Mississippi." The steamer developed important ties to Arkansas trade. On January 1, 1876, Hicks contracted with the Little Rock Railroad to handle all cotton and seed brought into Hopefield, Arkansas for shipment to New Orleans at 75 cents per bale. A like contract existed with two railroads serving Chicot City.

Along with a huge cargo capacity *Mary Bell* became known for luxury appointments. One observer offered the following description. "Ascending a handsome and commodious pair of stairs, the cabin is reached, certainly one of the most elegant ever constructed. It is surrounded by expensive promenades

and strikes the beholder at once as the embodiment of luxury and comfort. The pantry, barber shop, saloons, storerooms, and kitchen are in keeping with the rest of the boat. The colored cabin in the rear of the texas [is a] marvel of elegance." In this following observation the reporter performed a verbal sleight-of-hand for Jim Crow. "A special feature of the colored people's quarters is that no white person is allowed to enter them, thus guaranteeing this class of passengers the select privacy enjoyed by the whites. The tableware is of the heaviest plated silver, and is of very superior quality, as is everything connected with the culinary department. The cabin is noticeable for its glossy finish and snowy whiteness. The chandeliers are the chief attraction, especially when lighted up. The furniture is of the latest pattern and finish and has been much admired by all who have examined it. Taken as a whole, the *Mary Bell* is the most complete steamboat that ever floated up the Mississippi."

On March 3, 1876, the Vicksburg *Herald* announced that this "most complete steamboat" departed Memphis for New Orleans, but never made it past Vicksburg, Mississippi. A reporter provided this account of the boat's demise. "Shortly after noon the leviathan steamer steamed into port with a large cargo of cotton, her decks lined with passengers, and her band playing gaily. She landed at the cotton yard below the elevator and was visited by a great many Vicksburgians. When the boat arrived she had already in her cabin 163 passengers, which was all she had accommodations for in that quarter. It was therefore rendered necessary for the Vicksburgers to take quarters in the texas, the officers giving up their staterooms for the accommodation of the passengers. Some 40 or 50 people were added here. Many left the boat soon after she landed to walk or drive around the city. There were three bridal parties on the boat, and music, mirth, and dancing were the order from the time the boat left Memphis.

"The change came suddenly. About half past two o'clock in the afternoon, smoke was seen issuing from among the cotton bales directly under the baggage room, a little aft of the steps. A few sacks of cotton seed were pulled out, and the fire displayed itself but did not appear to be at all dangerous, as it was thought a few buckets of water could quickly extinguish it. One of the gentlemen who saw the fire went quickly into the cabin and whispered to the clerk, 'The boat is on fire.' Although he merely whispered this intelligence and was anxious to avoid creating a panic among the passengers, some of them noticed the pallor of his face and suspected danger and were quickly on the alert. The pilot ran to his post and blew the signal of distress. The bells rang, and the greatest excitement prevailed. The ladies hardly had time to realize their danger when they were caught hold of by friends and urged to leave the boat. Within two or three minutes after the alarm the stairway caught fire, and the flames and smoke descended into the cabin. Half a dozen or so [persons] ran down the steps and reached the shore by means of the stage plank, but they had hardly done so before the stairway was in flames.

"The stairway in flames, all egress by that route was cut off. Luckily the Parisot Line steamer *Tallahatchie* was lying between the burning steamer and the shore, loaded with cotton, which she was discharging on the *Mary Bell*, and the passengers of the burning steamer, by jumping over the guards onto the *Tallahatchie*, were afforded a means of escape. Very fortunately, the first effort to pull the *Tallahatchie* out from the perilous position was unsuccessful, and she remained there until everybody had gotten ashore, the wind blowing to the larboard and carrying the flames away from her. Another Parisot Line steamer, the *Yazoo* laid on the larboard side of the *Mary Bell,* transferring cotton to her, and was pulled away by the tug and permitted to drift down the river out of danger. One of the passengers, after seeing his wife ashore, started to go back after their baggage when he discovered the heavy stage reaching from the top of the cotton pile on the steamer to the bank was surrounded by flames and passage impossible.

"Not more than seven minutes had elapsed after the fire was discovered until the whole boat was enveloped in flames, and it was impossible in that short space of time to give much attention to anything else than saving human lives. A number of men passengers passed women and children over to other parties on the *Tallahatchie*, whence they were taken ashore. One of the pilots, who had gone to his post at the first cry of fire and was blowing the signal of distress remained at his post until the texas had caught fire, and to save himself had to jump over the texas roof and thence to the burning cotton on the guards. So far as could be ascertained [there was] no loss of life.

"The fire department answered the summons of the alarm bells with promptness, and all the fire steamers were quickly on the scene with heavy streams of water plying on the burning boat. Their efforts were unavailing. The cotton and seed burned like so much shavings saturated with oil, and when the fire reached the cabin it swept up almost in a moment. The whole boat, with the exception of the hull and its cargo, appeared to be one mass of flames. The size and shape of the bales of cotton were clearly defined and glowed like great lumps of fire. The whole area and neighborhood of the burning boat was covered by people watching the progress of the flames. The *Mary Bell* was the largest boat ever built for western waters, being of 4,000 tons burden, and having a capacity for over 10,000 bales of cotton as demonstrated on one trip when she carried into New Orleans the equivalent of 12,000 bales. The total loss of the boat and cargo will not fall short of $500,000, while the loss of the passengers in baggage, jewelry, and money can hardly be estimated. Very few of them saved anything, while many lost heavily in diamonds and costly jewelry. As flames consumed his vessel, Hicks watched the spectacle and admitted, 'Never will I give another steamboat a name commencing with an M. I'm not superstitious, but a strange fatality seems to follow the boats so named. I'll never do so again.'" (Way, 311.)

Arkansas Steamboat Landings

Author Fred W. Allsopp provides the names of many Delta riverboat landings in his *Folklore of Romantic Arkansas*, Vol. II (New York: The Grollier Society, 1931), 151-153. The following entries have connections to the Delta.

On the Mississippi River: Barfield Point, Plum Point, Osceola, Pecan Point, Hopefield, Walnut Bend, mouth of the St. Francis, Helena, Laconia, Montogomery's Point, mouth of the White, Napoleon, Cypress Creek, Arkopolis, Luna, Columbia, Sunnyside, Barnard's, and mouth of the Red River.

On the St. Francis River: Linden, Madison, Andrew's, Green Plains, and Wittsburg.

On the Lower White River: Wild Goose, Prairie, La Greux, Ox Bow, Scrub Grass, foot of Little Island, head Little Island, Big Creek, foot and head of Big Island, St. Charles, Anderson's Bluff, Maddox's Bay, Crockett's Bluff, Adam's Bluff, Casco, Aberdeen, Walnut Ridge, Clarendon, Warsaw, Crooked Point Bayou, Miller's Bluff, Arkopola, Devalls Bluff, Surrounded Hill, Buena Vista, Hidden Bluff, Little Hill, John Wright's, Wattensaw, Trimble Island, Des Ark, Lost Hill, Pryor's Woodyard, Augusta, Dudley's Dread, Rock Roe, Petit Glaize, Village Creek, Elizabeth, Jacksonport, and Reed's Bar.

On the Lower Arkansas River: Napoleon, Booties, Como, Notrebe, Arkansas Post, Silver Lake, Red Fork, Mound Grove, South Bend, Gum Point, Sample, Fairdale, Auburn, Mud Lake, Trotter, Upper Swan Landing, Governor Clayton, Gascony, Sycamore, Trulock's, Rob Roy, Cottonwood, Desruisseaux, Yell's, Mount Pleasant, Adamsburg, White Bluff, Plum Bayou, Barraques, Wampoo, Pawpaw, Eagle, Fourche, Old River, Badgetts, Dick Scruggs, Dick Fletcher, Peach Orchard, Churchill, Little Rock.

Port of Little Rock circa 1832. Arkansas River Historical Society.

Cigarette Landing

The story of riverboats introduces readers to a collection of fascinating peculiarities along regional rivers—-the names of landings and locations. Luna, Wild Goose, Crooked Point, Wild Haw, and many other strange names signified steamboat stops. Though the sources for many of these designations have been lost, a September 14, 1951, Memphis *Commercial Appeal* retrospective explained how one got its whimsical identity. Skipper of the steamer *Swain*, Captain Powell told this story: "We were heading down river from Memphis one day and passing the head of Island No. 40 on its Arkansas side when a quarter of a mile below us we saw two or three wagonloads of household plunder close to a timber opening along the river. Naturally, we on the boat believed it was a shipment for us. So we made ready to go in at an open timber spot. Just when the pilot on watch was figuring where was the best place to land, we saw the wagons pull out along a road leading to the center of the island. We had turned toward the middle of the river, knowing the shipment was not for us, when suddenly a young girl ran to the river embankment and hailed us.

"Our pilots saw her and at once signaled the engineer to slow down for it was necessary to make a quick turn to the island. Well, there was good water and we eased in rather slow. I was on the hurricane deck and walked toward the front after signaling the pilot to stop the power, because I thought if there was a freight pile for us we might find it below or above the point we had selected to land. When close in, I called out to the young girl, asking what was wanted. She made no answer, so I decided to go in where she was standing, and when we touched shore and put out a headline I asked her what she had to ship. 'Nothing' she answered. 'I just want to buy a package of cigarets.' That answer almost floored me, but I sent the cigarets ashore by a porter. She paid him. Then I asked the young girl's name. She answered: 'Miss Anna May Poudert and my father grows many bales of cotton every year. He ships to Memphis. So being without cigarets, I decided to hail your boat and buy a package. I'm greatly obliged, captain,' she said, disappearing behind some underbrush that lined the island's shore, just above and below the opening." The location became "a paying landing" on Island No. 40 [for] captains of Valley Line steamers, including Captain Powell, who named it Cigarette Landing. "That name stuck through all the years as packets went up and down the Mississippi River along the Arkansas side of Island 40."

An etching by Alfred Waud depicts would-be passengers hailing a steamboat.
This illustration appeared in the September 16, 1871, edition of *Every Saturday*.

Boats Built, Destroyed, or Noteworthy: 1876

Alberta: sternwheel packet (1876) operated in the White River. (Way, 9.)

Batesville: When this *Batesville* stopped at a woodyard on the White River, several country folks went on board to have a look. In order to impress them a member of the crew "opened a tune on the boat's calliope." Huddleston describes the consequences. It caused a "general stampede among the pioneers, frightening one of them so badly that he jumped in the river and waded out, instead of going out on the stage plank." When last heard of, "he was fifty miles from the woodyard, still wading over rocks, snakes, and lizards as fast as his legs would carry him, and shouting to the top of his voice, 'Old Gabriel's down at the woodyard with a lot of devils, blowing his horn for sinners to get from these diggings!'" (Huddleston, 85.)

Blufff City: The Pittsburgh *Gazette* on January 25, 1876, reported that this steamer struck a snag near Lauratown, Arkansas about 100 miles above Jacksonport, Arkansas on the Black River and "will likely prove a total loss."

City of Quincy: steamer (1871) sank during severe weather in February 1876 at Hardin's Point a few miles above Helena, Arkansas. While coming upstream its pilot could not control the boat. As a result, it struck a log and sank in about four minutes. The captain blew distress signals and flashed lights in an effort to attract *Idlewild*, which was blown ashore nearby. That vessel dispatched a yawl, but owing to the storm's fury, the dark night, and a raging current, that rescue attempt failed. *Idlewild* went to *City of Quincy* when the storm abated and took off passengers and 100 sacks of coffee. The wrecked steamer was "torn to pieces" by a fast-rising river. (Tippitt, 1876, 2.)

Dispatch: exploding boilers destroyed it at the mouth of the White River in October 1876. (Tippitt, 1876, 3, 11.)

Fanny Moore: completed in September 1876 for use in the Arkansas River. Named for a regional planter's daughter, it hit a bank at Sarassa, Arkansas about 50 miles below Pine Bluff in April 1877. (Tippitt, 1876, 4.)

Fort Gibson No. 2: Arkansas River packet reportedly sunk at Bayou Meto, Arkansas about 70 miles up the Arkansas River. (Tippitt, 1876, 4.)

Governor Garland: sternwheel packet (1876) built for Memphis & Pine Bluff Mail Line, but carried cotton on the Arkansas River. It burned in March 1877 at Red Fork, Arkansas. Three deckhands and one passenger died; boat a total loss. (Tippitt, 1876, 5.)

Grand Republic: steamer (1876) departed in April from St. Louis, Missouri with a cabin full of people and about 2,700 tons of freight destined for New Orleans. A newspaper there reported that crewmen stacked cotton bales 11 tiers high on the forecastle, from two to three tiers on the roof, and everywhere on the boat that space was found to store it. Such success would be limited since in September 1877 a fire consumed the steamer at St. Louis, Missouri along with *Carondelet*. From a September 21 Cairo, Illinois *Bulletin*: "News of the burning of *Grand Republic* and *Carondelet* the night before last created profound surprise and regret. It is probable there will never be another *Grand Republic*. The magnificence of her cabin will never be equaled again. The Pride of the Western Waters is gone and gone to stay."

Grand Tower: sidewheel packet (1870) became during May 1876 the fastest boat between Helena, Arkansas and Memphis. It set a record of six hours and 12 and one-half minutes. Unfortunately, the steamer burned in June 1876 after colliding with *Shippers' Own* at Goose Island below Commerce, Missouri. (Way, 197.)

Miami: One of Arkansas's most famous entertainment families made up the Ashley Band, a group initially consisting of slaves owned by the Ashley family. Nathan Warren and his children formed this company of gifted musicians and entertainers. After the Civil War original members and their descendants performed throughout the region. According to author Margaret Smith Ross, while returning from a Memphis event aboard *Miami* in 1876 the steamer exploded about six miles above Napoleon, Arkansas. Four family members died, and only two escaped the calamity.[144]

Osceola: sternwheel packet (1874) went down in February 1876 at Peters landing approximately 40 miles below Memphis while upbound from the St. Francis River with 300 bales. *City of Augusta* picked up the vessel's stranded passengers, and *Ella* took off its cotton. *T. F. Eckert* raised the steamer, and in June 1877 a resurrected *Osceola* went up the Yellowstone River, a trip recorded by Way. "En route, near Glendive, Mont., a beautiful white stallion was spotted, and the boat was landed. In pursuit went a number of cowboys who had taken passage, and observing from the boat's deck was a preacher and family. During the two hours spent in pursuit of the nag a tornado came along and demolished the steamboat. Those who told the story were quick to add that the preacher's wife was red-headed, confirmation that a white horse, a preacher, and a red-headed woman on a steamboat bodes no good." (Way, 358-359.)

Pat Cleburne: steamer (1870) suffered a boiler explosion near Weston, Kentucky on the Ohio River during 1876 while alongside *Arkansas Belle. Belle* tied up to the bank after becoming disabled by a line of coal flats that fouled the starboard wheel. Following the *Cleburne* explosion that boat floated downriver and burned. *Belle* caught fire as well, but passengers and crew extinguished the flames and

The packet *Pat Cleburne* was recalled more than 50 years after its 1876 demise as "probably the finest that ever ran the Arkansas." Memphis *Commercial Appeal*, May 12, 1927. Lee Line Steamers, Riverboat History Photograph.

[144]Margaret Smith Ross, "Nathan Warren, A Free Negro of the Old South," Arkansas Historical Quarterly 15:1 (Spring 1956), 60-61.

took the dead and wounded to Evansville, Indiana. (Tippitt, 1876, 2.) Owners named *Pat Cleburne* to honor an Arkansan who Dougan calls "perhaps the finest brigade commander in the Confederacy." The general died during November 1864 in the battle of Franklin, Tennessee.[145] A May 12, 1927, edition of the Memphis *Appeal* ran a retrospective piece about this steamer, calling it "queen of the Arkansas River. She was a side-wheel boat with a delightfully furnished cabin. She was operated several years between Memphis, Pine Bluff, Arkansas and Little Rock. Many of the older generations recall this packet as probably the finest that ever ran the Arkansas. Fate decreed a tragic end for this boat." Several crewmen, including the captain, lost their lives attempting to save passengers, but 16 passengers perished as well.

Pine Bluff: sternwheel packet (1876) built at Little Rock for Little Rock-Fort Smith trade. It went under at Tindell's landing on the Arkansas River roughly 40 miles above Little Rock in February 1877. (Way, 372.)

Rhoda: sternwheel packet (1875) called a "dinky" sank in February 1876 between the mouth of the St. Francis River and Helena, Arkansas. (Tippitt, 1876, 8.)

Rosa Miller: sternwheel packet (1875) carried mail out of Pine Bluff, Arkansas until it struck a snag and went down in October 1876 at Swan Lake about 40 miles below Pine Bluff; a total loss. (Tippitt, 1876, 6.)

Russ Porter: built at Helena, Arkansas for St. Francis River trade. (Tippitt, 1876, 12.)

St. Francis Belle: Traveling from the White River to Memphis in January 1876 it grounded at Island No. 65 on the Mississippi River. Water fell out from under the steamer, and it broke in two. (Tippitt, 1876, 13, 15.)

---

[145]Dougan, 215.

Roustabouts unloading cotton from a steamboat. Wikimedia.org.

Clerk at right checked shipments on and off, while deckhands at left handled freight aboard the steamboat.
Gandy and Gandy, Thomas H. Gandy from Henry C. Norman and Earl Norman negatives.

Always on Call

Chambermaids kept cabins clean and other cleaning necessary aboard steamboats.
Gandy and Gandy, Thomas H. Gandy from Henry C. Norman and Earl Norman negatives.

Though white workers sometimes performed menial tasks on steamboats, for the most part black employees filled those slots. Even before the Civil War ended slavery, planters sometimes leased their enslaved laborers to steamboat lines. Blacks wanted to get aboard steamers because work on them allowed more personal liberty, opportunities to locate family members sold down the river, and better chances to escape. Those who lacked the opportunity to serve aboard a vessel legally sometimes chose another route. Gudmestad shares the story of one enslaved person from Arkansas who "waded forty miles through swamps before stowing away on a steamer" during an escape attempt.[146] Steamboat employment opportunities had limits, however. Freedmen could not serve as officers because they sometimes had to admonish passengers who broke rules, and southern passengers would not take orders from them. In most situations black workers held jobs no one else wanted.

Gudmestad describes the difficulties associated with several employee positions. Stewards supervised the service staff on boats and had to be diplomatic with fussy patrons while handling their demands and complaints no matter how unreasonable. Cooks went to work in the morning's wee hours to prepare food for cabin passengers and crew, which could number hundreds of hungry people. They worked 18-hour days preparing gourmet meals to maintain a steamer in the "best boats" category. Waiters set up dining tables for cabin passengers

---

[146]Gudmestad, 144.

complete with place settings and served food and drink. After a meal ended they bussed dishes and took down tables before completing other tasks and bringing out the tables again to repeat the food service ritual. Porters carried luggage onto the vessel and stowed it in a baggage room on the boiler deck. They took care of personal property belonging to cabin passengers and unloaded luggage at destinations. Porters also helped waiters tend to stoves that heated cabins and assisted with cleaning saloons. Chambermaids tended to washing, ironing, and cleaning. At the bottom of a steamboat ladder stood cabin boys who handled "disagreeable tasks."

Passengers expected cabin crew members to be presentable and pleasing at all times. Stewards and waiters sported clean white shirts and sometimes white coats. Chambermaids wore long cotton dresses and aprons. That most employees in menial tasks were of "African descent reinforced white assumptions that God created blacks to serve them." Stewards, waiters, porters, and chambermaids always were on call. Though most of these jobs offered little thanks and lots of hard work, none of them compared to the responsibilities of firemen. They struggled continuously with shovels to feed fires necessary to propel a steamer. Men performed this task in an area filled with intensely hot air. To make matters more difficult, firemen worked for engineers who sometimes issued orders in a "blasphemous rage." Pilothouse bells connected to the engine room might signal in rapid succession orders to stop, back up, or move ahead slowly. This could be disconcerting and highly irritating. Additionally, firemen knew that they were only a boiler explosion away from eternity. One engineer claimed to fear Heaven "because he would encounter all the people he had killed in boiler explosions."[147]

---

[147]Gudmestad, 36-38.

Boats Built, Destroyed, or Noteworthy: 1877

Alberta: sternwheel packet (1876). One of the first strikes by steamboat personnel on the White River occurred in September 1877 when *Alberta* deckhands held out for higher wages. Dissatisfied with the $20 per month pay for working four days each week, they insisted on a raise. Though results of the strike are unknown, *Alberta* lost little traveling time on the White River during that month, according to the Batesville *Guard* on September 13, 1877.

Archie P. Green: sternwheel packet (1873) advertised for White River-Batesville trade. *Green* joined several other vessels in February 1877 to celebrate a Jacksonport, Arkansas Mardi Gras. One afternoon several decorated steamers pulled up to the town dock carrying merrymakers from various river towns taking advantage of half fare excursion rates. On the morning of February 13, King Peter Bee embarked at Newport, Arkansas and arrived at Jacksonport on a bedecked procession of steamboats, including *Ruth*, picked to be the flotilla's flagship, followed by *Batesville, Alberta, Arch P. Green, McArthur, Music,* and *Duck.* (Huddleston, 86.) *Archie P. Green* sank approximately three miles below Batesville, Arkansas with cotton cargo during February 1880.

Florence Meyer: sternwheel packet (1876) en route from Fort Smith, Arkansas to New Orleans struck a snag and went down at Petit Jean's landing approximately 90 miles from Little Rock; a total loss. (Tippitt, 1877, 4.)

General Pierson: sidewheeler (1876) transferred Memphis and Little Rock Railroad cars across the Mississippi River. In April 1892, while caught in a windstorm at Hopefield, Arkansas, it blew across the river and lost both stacks plus its wheelhouse. The steamer sank at Memphis during 1906 or later. (Way, 182.)

Granger: packet constructed in 1874 for "short trades" on the Arkansas River. It burned about four miles above Little Rock in July 1877. (Way, 197.)

Hattie B. Nowland: sternwheel packet (1877) ran a Little Rock-Memphis route until lost in May 1880 at Cooper's landing on the Arkansas River. It broke in two, and the hull filled with sand. (Way, 208.)

Katie Hooper: sternwheel packet (1877) in October 1878 loaded at Cincinnati, Ohio for an Arkansas River run. It crashed into a wrecked *Hattie Nowland* on the Arkansas River and was destroyed. (Way, 268.)

Low Water: snagged at Madison, Arkansas on the St. Francis River in March 1877. (Way, 296.)

Mary Elizabeth: steamer (1877) departed Cincinnati, Ohio for Pine Bluff, Arkansas during January 1878 for Arkansas River trade. (Tippitt, 1878, 10.)

Milt Harry: sternwheel packet (1877) burned on the White River approximately 120 miles above Batesville, Arkansas in March 1885. (Way, 322.)

T. N. Cligg: built at Pine Bluff, Arkansas during 1877. (Way, 498.)

W. A. King: built at Van Buren, Arkansas in 1877. (Way, 499.)

Fever Overtakes *John Porter*

A steamer *John Porter* monument at Gallapolis, Ohio. Plymale Family in America Family Tree website.

Events aboard *John Porter* indicate the disastrous effects Yellow Fever had on one steamer. After departing New Orleans during July 1878 a crewman died from the disease. This news spread rapidly up and down the river, and the boat was not allowed to land until August 19, when machinery problems forced it to shore about three miles below Gallapolis, Ohio. By then 23 of the steamer's 31-man crew were dead, and the fever spread to Gallapolis. Authorities burned barges towed by *John Porter,* and after fumigation the boat proceeded to Pittsburgh, Pennsylvania. Unable to find work because of the boat's reputation, Captain John Porter sold it. The new owner renamed the steamer *Sidney Dillon* and made several changes in appearance. It operated until 1895 when the boat burned at Sedamsville, Ohio. (Tippitt, 1878, 8.)

Bronze John Arrives

During the 1800s diseases often travelled on rivers, and Memphis became a frequent destination. In fall 1878 a devastating strain of Yellow Fever borne by mosquitoes ravaged that city, and the plague eventually killed about 18,000 people in the Mississippi Valley. Mosquitoes that produced periodic regional epidemics flourished in temperatures ranging from 70 to 90 degrees. They preferred to lay their eggs in still water and feed on blood. After contamination, victims became sick in three to six days, and the disease caused fevers in excess of 100 degrees, nausea, intense headaches, delirium, vomiting of coagulated blood, and yellow skin. This discoloration led to the disease's nickname — Bronze John. During the 1878 epidemic about 25 percent of Memphis's infected people died. The fever initially came from Africa to the Americas on slave ships, an interesting irony, and at first spread throughout the Caribbean and Central America. It acquired the name Yellow Fever because of yellow quarantine flags designating its presence at locations. Though eventually spreading to many U. S. cities, author Jeanette Keith explains that Americans "came to associate the fever with the Gulf Coast in general, but especially with New Orleans," a city often victimized by diseases.[148]

Like many things that arrived in New Orleans, the virus went upriver on steamboats that unloaded infected people in states along the way, including Arkansas. From landings and port towns they travelled inland by train and other means, spreading the disease as they went. Fortunately, military doctors in 1901 identified a connection between this virus and mosquitoes and developed effective treatments. A graphic and touching account of suffering caused by the disease comes from a Memphis survivor. Mary Harris Jones describes the experience in her autobiography. "The dead surrounded us. They were buried at night quickly and without ceremony. All about my house I could hear weeping and the cries of delirium. One by one, my four little children sickened and died. I washed their little bodies and got them ready for burial. My husband caught the fever and died. I sat alone through nights of grief. No one came to me. No one could. Other homes were as stricken as was mine. All day long, all night long, I heard the grating of the wheels of the death cart."[149]

---

[148]Jeanette Keith, *Fever Season. The story of a terrifying epidemic and the people who saved a city* (New York: Bloomsbury Press, 2012), 7. The 1878 flu epidemic was one of the 19th Century's greatest disasters. The disease killed more than 18,000 persons along the Lower Mississippi River in only a few months. In Memphis the death toll came to about 5,000 residents.This would be the contemporary equivalent of one million New Yorkers dying in a plague.

[149]Mary Harris Jones, *Autobiography of Mother Jones*, Mary Field Parton, editor (Chicago: Charles H. Kerr & Co., 1925), 1. Despite this horrifying account, some doctors and other Memphians became heroes for their care of those suffering from the disease. However, the crisis created cowards as well. They turned away from desperate people and fled the city.

Boats Built, Destroyed, or Noteworthy: 1878-1879

Chas. P. Choteau: After modified and enlarged in St. Louis, Missouri during March 1878 it made many trips south picking up commodities along the Delta for St. Louis-New Orleans trade. During semi-monthly service from Memphis the steamer hauled thousands of bales of Arkansas cotton. In 1882 it landed at New Orleans with almost 9,000 bales, a "blue ribbon" run. The New Orleans *Times* on November 23, 1887, reported what happened on the boat's last journey. "The *Chas. P. Choteau,* while lying at Sunflower Landing, at 7 p.m. had taken on some cotton. Captain Thorwegan rang the last bell to back out and went into the cabin for supper. Misses Carrie and Sophia Sliger, passengers, walked forward on the boiler deck and discovered the fire burning. They went to the cabin and told the captain. General alarm was given, but owing to the wind the flames spread so rapidly that nothing could be done to check them, and nothing was saved." A fireman and one deck passenger died.

City of Augusta: sidewheel packet operated in White River-New Orleans trade during 1878. (Way 89.)

General Chas. H. Tompkins: sternwheel packet (1878) ran northern rivers until entering Arkansas River-Memphis trade. It went down about one-half mile above the mouth of the White River. (Way, 180.)

Hard Cash: in 1879 ran white River-Memphis trade. (Krivor, Final Report, Vol. I, 115.)

Jennie May: packet built in Fort Smith, Arkansas during 1879. (Way, 245.)

John Howard: sternwheel packet (1871). In fall 1879 this Batesville-New Orleans steamer "broke its hawser while dragging over a shoal below Augusta, [Arkansas]. A piece of the broken cable struck the mate, killing him instantly." (Huddleston, 92.)

John M. Chambers: in 1878 carried medical supplies from St. Louis to help people in Yellow Fever stricken towns along the Mississippi River. The Memphis *Appeal* on August 25, 1878, reported that the rescue vessel would "stop at every landing between here and Vicksburg, [Mississippi]."

Josie Harry: Completed in 1878, the steamer delayed its entry into trades until November due to the fever outbreak. W. C. Harry, father of the steamer's captain, died from the disease. During 1883 it sank in the Mississippi River about 15 miles below Memphis. (Tippitt, 1878, 16.)

Marlen Speed: sternwheel packet (1878) lost on the Arkansas River at Pleasants landing. (Way, 309.)

Picayune: According to the July 2, 1878, Pittsburgh *Gazette*, "They have a river craft at Pine Bluff (Ark.) called the *Picayune*. It is ready at all times to carry people or freight up and down the brown-colored Arkansas. She runs to Wildcat above and Swan Lake below Pine Bluff."

Rose City: sternwheel packet working Little Rock-Fort Smith trade in 1878. (Way, 402.)

Trader: headed for the White River in August 1879, but had to turn back, supposedly because its master was arrested for violating quarantine orders. (Huddleston, 92.)

Warner: From the Memphis *Appeal* on May 2, 1878: "At 9:20 this morning a steamboat was observed steaming up the river along the Arkansas shore nearly opposite Fort Pickering [at Memphis]. Those on the bluff beheld the steamboat and barges enveloped in a white cloud of smoke and steam. The vessel commenced to float down the stream, and as the smoke and steam cleared away *Warner* was observed to go down suddenly, bow foremost, her stern seemed to rise up and plunge downward, while her cabin commenced floating away on fire. The barges which the *Warner* was towing were seen to be on fire also, and confusion among those on board was clearly apparent. Men were seen leaping into the river and onto the barges. A mass of timber forced high into the air by the explosion of the boilers was seen falling all around them. The *Warner* was en route to St. Louis, having left New Orleans a week ago."

Winnie: started up the White River in September 1879, but broke its lines while jumping a shoal at McGuire's, between Newport and Batesville, Arkansas. It could go no farther, so the crew unloaded freight and returned to Newport. (Huddleston, 92.)

J. M. White

J. M. White: With great expectations of freight income, owners launched this third version of *J. M. White* in April 1878. Though built to suit Captain John Tobin, he expressed buyer's remorse and called the steamer too large and costly to operate. His cash flow problem eventually disappeared in a cloud of smoke. On December 15, 1886, the New Orleans *Picayune* announced that "*J. M. White* caught fire [at] 10:30 p.m. last night while at Blue Store Landing, Pt. Coupee Parish, Louisiana and was destroyed. She had 3,600 bales of cotton, 8,000 sacks of seed, and 400 barrels of oil. It is estimated that 15 or 20 persons were lost. The fire originated near the boilers. One of the mates on shore superintending loading of cotton discovered the fire. He gave the alarm and rushed to the cabin to awaken the passengers. The engineer's crew immediately attacked the fire with their hose."

In a special to the new Orleans *Picayune* from Bayou Sara the newspaper offered more details, some of which varied from the previous account. "The *White* burned at St. Maurice Landing, five miles above Bayou Sara on the right bank at 10:15 p.m. last night. Pilot R. H. Smith was on watch and hastened below to awaken his partner, J. S. Stout. Both had to jump into the river and cling to cotton bales to reach the shore. The fire spread with great rapidity. It is thought to have been started by carelessness by a deck passenger. The *White* was completely destroyed in less than 15 minutes. A number of cabin passengers and deck passengers were trapped on stern by fire, and leaped into the river, and were lost." (Tippitt, 1878, 1-5A.)

Floating Opulence

These photos illustrate luxurious accommodations aboard *J. M. White*. The steamer's opulence led a reporter to pen the following ditty. "Aladdin built a palace, He built it in a night. And Captain Tobin bought it, and named it *J. M. White*."[150] Observers called the boat "a supreme triumph in cotton boat architecture." An article in the August 7, 1878, *Louisville Courier- Journal* described the vessel's cabin. "The style of the architecture of the cabin will have to be seen to have any idea of, as it was not taken out of the books; nor was it got up to be like anything as ever been built before."

[150]Gandy and Gandy, 3.

Henry Frank, was built expressly to haul cotton in the Memphis-New Orleans trade. On April 2, 1881, it carried 9,226 bales, the largest load ever handled by a packet. It also carried 250 tons of other cargo. From the James E. York Postcard Collection.

Str. JENNIE HOWELL with
2,456 bales cotton
Jan. 1873

Jennie Howell serviced the White and Arkansas rivers. This photo illustrates the enormous amount of cotton sometimes packed aboard such vessels. Downs Collection.

End of an Era

Though the 1870s may have marked the high tide of steamboat grandeur, many owners went under water financially. Gould cites several contributing factors. Some steamboat operators initially hired keelboat men to staff their complicated vessels, and many of these men eventually became masters and pilots. Their lack of management skills doomed the fortunes of their boats. Another cause involved financial leverage. Gould points out that during the decade "a company, or even an individual, who represented any unencumbered real estate could easily secure sufficient credit to build a steamboat without any money." However, financial leverage doth giveth, and doth taketh away. Undercapitalized owners throughout the Mississippi Valley "lost their homes, their farms, and their all, by pledging them to pay for building a steamboat they had no use for." Additionally, "what was still more demoralizing, this was often done by men who had no knowledge of the business, nor in fact of any business."[151] Another contributing factor continued to be the danger in navigating regional rivers and the resulting high cost of insurance. Rates were "so high that no price could be charged sufficient to pay the carrier a profit after paying" for insurance and other expenses. Boat owners declined to insure "when they felt at all able to take the risk themselves."[152]

Gould also points out that technical failures produced financial failure as well, such as boiler explosions, failed machinery, or escaping steam, typically uninsurable mishaps. Owners depended on the boat's engineers to see that these malfunctions did not occur, but not all engineers were created equal. Some of the disasters were attributable to too much whisky and too much steam. An additional issue brought up by the author goes to the bottom line. It was "the loose, unsystematic manner of doing business. The few well known good businessmen that have engaged in river transportation from time to time have been unable to exercise sufficient influence over the great majority to introduce and maintain such systems and principles of business as will alone insure success in any business."[153]

Though mismanagement, exorbitant operating costs, and disasters plagued steamboat trades in the late 1800s, railroads ran over many of them. Hunter explains that southern rail lines "hitherto serving as feeders to the river reversed this role" after obtaining connections with major cities. For example, "A railroad tapping the Arkansas Valley gave Pine Bluff and Little Rock rail connections to New Orleans and undercut steamboat operations on the Arkansas River." By the mid 1880s almost all towns on the Lower Mississippi with a population of more than 1,000 offered a rail connection with New Orleans, Memphis, or St Louis, Missouri.[154] Gudmestad observes that in their prime, steamboats created sensual experiences in a glittery world, but in the 1880s they were "merely pre-war steamers caked with layers of dirt. Steamers were dying of neglect.[155] Gandy and Gandy describe the end of the steamboat era. "As the Twentieth Century was born, steam boating began to die. Powerful diesel boats had begun to dominate river transportation,"[156] and much steamboat history became myth.

---

[151]Gould, 580.

[152]Gould, 581.

[153]Gould, 581-582.

[154]Hunter, 589.

[155]Gudmestad, 175.

[156]Gandy, 3.

Boats Built, Destroyed, or Noteworthy: 1880-1899

Alberta No. 2: After departing Jacksonport en route to Newport, Arkansas during November 1883 fire destroyed this vessel. Huddleston commends Captain John T. Warner who "bravely remained at the wheel until the fiery inferno finally forced him to jump through the opening in the front of the pilothouse. The heroic engineer stayed in the engine room until communications with Captain Warner were severed, then he also jumped overboard." Both captain and engineer survived, but a young watchman "fought the fire until the very last" and perished. (Huddleston, 97.)

Alberta No. 3: built in 1884 for White River trade. While on the Lower White River during October 1887, cotton bales on the freight deck caught fire as the vessel neared Indian Bay. Crew and passengers survived, but apparently not Captain Wilmont Gibbes. (Way, 9.)

Alda: (1891) originally registered for passengers and freight, but in June 1908 lost its passenger license. The steamer became a towboat during 1909-1910 and made almost 50 trips between Clarendon, Arkansas and White River logging camps. (Krivor, Final Report, Vol. I.)

A. R. Bragg: sternwheel packet (1890) built at Newport, Arkansas for use on the White, Black, and Current rivers. (Way, 3.) The vessel sank in January 1893 at the head of Padgett's Island in the White River several miles below Batesville, Arkansas. Salvagers raised *Bragg*, reparied it, and returned the boat to Black Rock – Newport trade. (Huddleston, 107.)

Austin Corbin: A steamer named for its owner, Austin Corbin, who purchased plantations in Chicot County, Arkansas during the late 1800s. By 1895 his steamer docked at Sunnyside Landing at Lake Chicot. Corbin became controversial when he imported Italian immigrants to farm his vast acreage. This led to a federal peonage investigation.

Bedford: provided weekly packet service between the Lower White River and New Orleans during the early 1880s.

Birdie Bailey: sternwheel packet (1885) built at Little Rock for Arkansas River-Memphis trade. It went down after running into a snag on the Yazoo River in Mississippi. (Way, 54.)

Blue Wing: sternwheel packet (1882) originally named *Fannie Freese*. The vessel sank at Craighead Point roughly 16 miles below Osceola, Arkansas on the Mississippi River in September 1894. (Way, 56.)

Border City: sternwheel packet built at Fort Smith, Arkansas in 1885. (Way, 58.)

Buckeye State: sternwheel packet (1883) burned at Barfield Point, Arkansas during January 1901; one casualty. (Way, 63.)

C. B. Reese: transferred from the Arkansas River to the White River in 1883-1884 where it removed 302 snags and six drift piles. An engineer report indicates that the crew cut down 1,318 trees along the shore to prevent them from falling into the river and obstructing navigation. (Krivor, Final Report, Vol. I, 132.)

C. N. Kraft: sternwheel packet (1882) sank about eight miles above Little Rock in the Arkansas River during October 1886. (Way, 66.)

C. R. Cummings: sternwheel packet (1893) operated between Shreveport, Louisiana and Fulton, Arkansas. (Way, 66.)

Caddo: sternwheel packet (1890) built at Arkadelphia, Arkansas. (Way, 67.)

Carrie S. Douglas: possibly a ferry (1883) built at Morrilton, Arkansas. (Way, 74.)

Chickasaw: in November 1883 departed Memphis on its first trip up the White River. The boat had "newfangled electric lights," and Captain Warner described them and their effect on man and beast ashore. The November 13, 1938, *Arkansas Gazette* told his story. "They were so bright they hurt my eyes. The first night we came up White River" with *Chickasaw* illuminating the shoreline, and "it created panic with the beasts of the forest. I'd see the lantern-like eyes of some wild animal shining from a limb of a tree. I'd turn that light on him, and man alive, what a racket the creature made getting away." The lights also shocked a church congregation. "The first place I saw after leaving Indian Bay was a Negro church. I switched on the searchlight, then trained it on the church. I never saw so many people running from a place of worship as fast in my life. They tumbled over each other." When the boat pulled into a nearby landing, the preacher approached this mysterious vessel. A member of the crew urged him to bring his congregation aboard and have a look, and he did.

Chickasaw: Another *Chickasaw* became part of a string of disasters at a Memphis wharf. While deckhands unloaded fuel coal from a flat tied up to the packet's port side, chaos unfolded. A February 13, 1890, Memphis *Appeal* reported the incident: "A large tree came floating down the current, its projecting limbs being in front and its root up stream. The current carried it toward the flat. It struck the flat on its larboard (port) side, crushing a hole eighteen inches square in its larboard bow . . . and the coal flat began to sink." To prevent harm to the steamer, a *Chickasaw* mate cut lines to the coal flat. It floated downstream where it rammed and destroyed two barges before sinking.

Chicot: packet (1889) transported mail and passengers between Greenville, Mississippi and Arkansas City, Arkansas on the Mississippi River. (Way, 85.)

Choctaw: sternwheel packet (1899) built at Dardanelle, Arkansas and initially used on the Arkansas River. (Way, 86.)

City of Idaho: sternwheel short trader (1898) working from Memphis to Fulton, Arkansas and Peters landing. It ran Newport-Clarendon trade on the White River during 1903. (Way, 92.)

City of Little Rock: in January 1898 hit a snag and sank in the Arkansas River.[157]

Dan Rice's Floating Opera House and Museum: An 1880 census indicates that only 317 people lived in Osceola, Arkansas that year. Despite an apparent scarcity of customers, *Dan Rice's Floating Opera House and Museum* tied up at the town dock. According to the Osceola *Times* on October 23, 1880, the showboat provided "delightful music, mirth, drama, and laughable pantomime."

Dean Adams: sidewheel packet constructed in 1880 for Arkansas City-Vicksburg trade. It burned at a Memphis wharf in 1886. (Way, 122.)

DeSoto: sidewheeler (1898) crushed by ice at Memphis in January 1918. The Thompson Brothers plantation in Arkansas acquired its roof bell. (Way, 126.)

Eli: sternwheel packet built at Little Rock during 1887. (Way, 144.)

Ella: sternwheel packet (1881) in Little Rock-Fort Smith trade during 1884. (Way, 146).

Elva: sternwheel ferry (1899) operated on the Arkansas River serving the Dardanelle & Russellville Railroad line. (Way, 147.)

Emma: sternwheel packet (1893) built at DeValls Bluff, Arkansas. (Way, 149.)

Eugene: sternwheel packet (1887) in Arkansas River-Memphis trade. (Way, 155.)

---

[157](From scrap book entries compiled by Tippitt, undated and not sourced. Hereafter referred to as Tippitt scrapbook.)

Loading Cotton

J. A. Woodson tied up at Colonel. V. Y. Cook's landing a few miles below Oil Trough, Arkansas to pick up cotton harvested at the Cook plantation. Built in 1881 this steamer operated in the White River from 1891 to 1896. Huddleston Steamboat Photograph Collection, UALR Center for Arkansas History and Culture.

Huddleston describes deckhands who became "masters" at loading bales, the 500-pound oblong blocks of compressed lint that fueled the Delta economy and sometimes fires that destroyed riverboats. The author says that "At some landings the bank was quite steep, steep enough that when a bale of cotton was placed on the bank end of the gangplank it would slide quickly to the boat deck. A deckhand holding the bale with a cotton hook would run behind the bale and control its speed and direction. Occasionally, rather than guiding it with his hook, a daring roustabout would ride a bale down. The bales didn't always slide straight, however, and if not guided could catch one of the cables that supported the gangplank. When that happened, any rider aboard the bale would find himself tossed into the river." (Huddleston, 36.)

Florence Meyer: On February 29, 1880, the New Orleans *Times* reported that the steamer departed New Orleans headed to Batesville, Arkansas with 25,000 sacks of salt and general merchandise. In September 1880 it sank about 12 miles above Natchez, Mississippi; five crew members died; cargo and vessel a total loss.

Four Boys: ferry built at Pine Bluff, Arkansas in 1882. (Way, 171.)

Freddie Robinson: this steamer (1882) temporarily replaced the wrecked *DeSmet* in White River trade; inspected through 1886 (Way, 173.)

F. W. Tucker: sternwheel packet (1897) built at Black Rock, Arkansas and operated on the White, Black, and Current rivers. (Way, 159.)

General Charles H. Tompkins: moved to the Lower White River from upriver in October 1891, but its service there proved to be short-lived. When about two miles up a White River chute in November of that year the boat hit a snag. Most of the cargo could not be saved, but a businessman bought the wreckage. (Huddleston, 104.)

George W. Decker: sternwheel packet constructed at Black Rock, Arkansas in 1885. (Way, 186.)

G. H. Van Etten: sternwheel packet (1881) built at Little Rock to haul freight from Little Rock and Pine Bluff to Rosedale, Arkansas on the Mississippi River. (Way, 175.)

G.M. Sively: sternwheel packet (1893). In fall 1901 it worked at Helena, Arkansas as a towboat during daytime and offered excursions at night. (Way, 175.)

G. W. Lyons: worked the White River during 1895 and 1896. (Krivor, Final Report, Vol. I, 117.)

G. W. Mayo: sternwheel packet (1888) built at Fort Smith, Arkansas and used on the Arkansas River until 1896. (Way, 176.)

Henry Sheldon: from December 1886 to January 1887 this snagboat removed 166 snags, 2,014 trees, and six drift piles from Newport, Arkansas to the mouth of the White River, according to an engineer report. (Krivor, Final Report, Vol. I, 132.)

Irma: sternwheel packet constructed at Little Rock during 1896 for Arkansas River short trades. (Way, 225.)

Jack Porter: ferry built at Little Rock in 1882. (Way, 238.)

James Lee: had the distinction of being the scene of a notorious lynching. Ben Patterson led black farm workers in a Crittenden County, Arkansas strike during September 1891 that resulted in the death of a white plantation manager. Chased by a mob seeking revenge for that killing and destruction of planter property, Patterson led his followers to Cat Island in the Mississippi River. They intended to board a riverboat and escape, but vigilantes found them and attacked the men, killing two and capturing nine. Patterson and another man escaped, but not for long. After boarding the steamer *James Lee* a mob found the strike leader and murdered him. Vigilantes lynched the captured strikers, and according to several editions of the Memphis *Commercial Appeal* from October 1 through 7, marauding whites victimized other black farm workers as well.

J. B. Galloway: (1899) employed in lumber trade on the White River until fall 1904. (Krivor, Final Report, Vol. I, 125.)

J. B. Woods: burned in December 1898 at Posey's on the Arkansas River. (Tippitt scrapbook.)

Joe Peters: considered to be one of the swiftest sternwheelers in White River trade during 1884-1885. (Krivor, Final Report, Vol. I, 115.)

John Matthews: destroyed after hitting a railroad bridge at Van Buren, Arkansas in June 1892. (Tippitt scrapbook.)

John R. Meigs: in September and October 1880 removed 270 snags, cut down 298 trees, and hauled off a wrecked coal barge at DeValls Bluff, Arkansas. In 1882 the snagboat continued work on the White River, according to an engineer report. (Krivor, Final Report, Vol. I, 131.)

Josie D. Harkins: fire destroyed this packet on the White River during June 1892. (Tippitt scrapbook.)

Josie Harry: In December 1883, while carrying White River cargo toward Memphis, it burned about 20 miles below the Bluff City. A Memphis *Commercial Appeal* retrospective edition on April 7, 1937, carried an eyewitness account of the disaster. "I heard the distress whistle of the *Josie Harry*. I saw her coming upriver, deep smoke almost hid the boat. Burning bales of cotton were being thrown overboard. Flames soon enveloped the beautiful steamer, and her hull drifting toward the middle of the river, sank."

Kate Adams: sidewheel packet (1882) built for Memphis-Arkansas City trade. Named for the wife of the boat's owner, *Kate* broke the speed record in 1883 for travel between Memphis and Helena, Arkansas. The boat burned 40 miles below Memphis at Commerce landing on Dec. 23, 1888, with 33 lives lost. Two successor *Kate Adams* were built (1888 and 1899) for Memphis-Arkansas City trade. (Way, 263-264.)

Lew Preston: ferry built at Pine Bluff, Arkansas in 1882. (Way, 284.)

Liberty: sternwheel packet (1889) went into White River-Memphis trade in 1896. At least five other vessels shared this name. (Way, 285.)

Lightwood: sternwheel packet constructed at Little Rock in 1884. The vessel was "long in U. S. Engineer service" on the White River and rebuilt at Little Rock in 1904. (Way, 286).

Lorna Doone: sternwheel packet built at Fort Smith, Arkansas in 1891. It "turned over on her

side" and sank in the St. Francis River during January 1900. (Way, 293.)

Louise Stecher: steam yacht built at Judsonia, Arkansas in 1893. (Way, 295.)

Luella Brown: sternwheel packet (1890) ran between Greenville, Mississippi and Luna, Arkansas. (Way, 299.)

Mark Twain: sternwheel packet (1872). Osceola, Arkansas became known as a shipping point for game killed by the region's numerous hunters. Boats carrying dead fowl and critters serviced Memphis markets. A November 25, 1882, edition of the Osceola newspaper announced that "Mr. W. E. Moss shipped 400 ducks last Tuesday on the steamer *Mark Twain*. In 1885 its boilers exploded killing two persons and destroying the boat. (Way, 308.)

Mary F. Carter: sternwheel packet built at Clarendon, Arkansas in 1893. During January 1896 it ran regularly on the White River. (Way, 312.)

Myrtle: sternwheel packet (1893) constructed at Yellville, Arkansas. It burned in March 1895 while heading to McBee's landing on the White River. (Way, 335.)

New Mary Morgan: sternwheel packet (1892) built at Little Rock. (Way, 345.)

New Mattie: sternwheeler (1886) entered White River-Memphis trade until destroyed on the White River after striking a riverbank in February 1900. The Memphis *Scimitar* reported on February 19 that "The *New Mattie* is a total wreck. She sank in White River en route to Memphis with 340 bales of cotton and 16 tons of hay on board. She made a forced landing at Wild Goose and disembarked her passengers, most of the crew were off when she went down and broke in two. The *Ora Lee* will be sent down after her freight."

Orlando: sternwheel packet (1891) sank after hitting a log during July 1901 about two miles above Peach Orchard Bluff on the White River. (Way, 358.)

Ozark Queen: sternwheel packet (1896) built in Batesville, Arkansas for service on the White River. It operated in Batesville-McBee's trade during May 1903. (Way, 360.)

Peerless: constructed at Little Rock in 1882. (Way, 365.)

Rock City: sternwheel packet (1897) went down in the St. Francis River about six miles from Jeffersonville, Arkansas during January 1900. (Way, 400.)

Rosa Bland: sternwheel packet built at Little Rock in 1889. (Way, 401.)

Roseville: sternwheel packet built at Ozark, Arkansas in 1891 and lost on the Arkansas River at Sandy Bayou Crossing. Another sternwheel packet named *Roseville* was constructed at Sparda, Arkansas in 1879. (Way, 403.)

S. P. Pond: worked the White River during 1895-1896. (Krivor, Final Report, Vol. I, 117.)

Wichita: sternwheel snagboat built at Little Rock in 1881 for use on the Arkansas River. (Way, 485-486.)

Wm. Druhe No. 2: sternwheel packet constructed at Fort Smith, Arkansas in 1890 for Arkansas River trade. (Way, 488.)

---

[158]Stewart-Abernathy, 39.

Port Eads

Port Eads: ran afoul of a Memphis bridge in 1890 while towing seven barges. Many riverboats crashed into bridges spanning major waterways in the late 1800s. These impediments proved to be a double threat to river commerce. They posed a hazard to boat navigation and increased the reach of railroad shipping that competed with riverboats. Impaired by fog, this steamer struck a bridge pier, and a February 11, 1890, Memphis *Weekly Avalanche* reported the consequences. "The engines were smashed and the furnaces knocked to pieces. The lower deck caught fire and when Pilot Townsend got his wife out of the cabin, a sheet of flame was pouring out of the front of the boat. The boat went to pieces immediately, and the freight barges drifted down the river, leaving the water around the pier black with fragments of the wreck, floating baggage and human beings battling for life in the icy current." Unfortunately, six crewmen died in the accident.

Several boat captains weighed in on the bridge controversy. In the February 13, 1890, Memphis *Appeal*, N. B. McNeeley argued that "I do not think the interests of the river should be made subservient to the rail." J. P. Daugherty explained in the same article that "The location of pier No. 2 has confined the current so that a boat rocks like a cradle in making the passage. She must keep a full head of steam on, and in the dark or fog the passage is absolutely dangerous." Additional bridges would be constructed connecting Memphis and Arkansas making passage even more tricky. Gould expressed his views about bridges in a March 1873 letter to the St. Louis *Democrat* quoted by Stewart-Abernathy. "The great mania for railroad building has entirely eclipsed the importance of river transportation." He complained that railroad companies place "obstructions in the channels of our great navigable streams that will do more to prevent barge and steamboat navigation, or cheap transportation, than all other causes combined."[158] Collisions between boats and bridges ranged up and down the Mississippi River for many years, but eventually improvements in each made room for both.

Brutish Outrage

White Water: The Batesville *Guard* of August 2, 1882, reported a "brutish outrage" that allegedly occurred aboard *White Water*. The story concerned warrants "sworn out" against a man whose name the newspaper did not release. He was accused of slander and "the grave charge of assault to commit rape. These warrants were sworn out by a young lady from Toledo, Ohio." She was on her way to Batesville, Arkansas to visit a sister when the incident occurred. While near McGuire's landing, "after repeated advances and repulses, the gentleman (?) of wealth followed the lady into her stateroom and locked the door, laid hands upon her and thrust her upon the bed, then and there attempted his fiendish design. The evidence is, the young lady used every endeavor to force him to desist, when fortunately for the young lady a violent rap at the door by Captain Byron Woodbury" ended the assault.

When the case reached court, "The plain statement of the lady upon the stand, her manner of testifying, her conduct before the court, are indelible evidence that an outrage was attempted upon her person." The defense presented testimony from two deckhands attacking the woman's virtue, but these men were charged with perjury. "Many false rumors regarding this lady have been silently afloat, arising from the conduct of [the accused man] towards her at the time and on the boat mentioned. At the trial this lady's virtue was vindicated, her chastity established to the satisfaction of everyone, and her conduct commended by every person who was present in the courtroom and heard her testify." An initial ruling found that "the evidence fully warranted the court in holding the defendant over on bond to answer at the next circuit court session."

Coda

Once upon a time, steamboats provided more than transportation. They were night dragons, lighting the sky with their flames in what could have been a fairy tale. Steamers competed in dramatic races. They offered luxury to those who could afford to cross the gangplank and travel first class. The culture they created is long gone and cannot be duplicated. We travel fast these days, and the trip is rarely what matters. It is a timely arrival, and what is between here and there often passes by in a blurred landscape. William Tippitt moved with a different rhythm, a river gait, and in the following reflections from his compendium he says why.

"Nothing compares to a ride on a steamboat," he says. "The old sidewheeler with the steady patter-patter-pat of her great wheels striking the water, the gentle rolling of the big boat as her cranks rolled over center, the slight surge of power as pistons moved out on another journey, the slow ripple through her hull as vibration traverses its length, all make an unforgettable experience. Exhaust switched into her stacks becomes a steady pulsating breath of power, muted softly as she settles down on her run. The steady plop-plop of a sternwheeler, with ever present vibration from her wheel, traversing from bottom to top, jiggling every piece of her, makes for the most pleasant sensation, a sense of power contained, a sense of well-being found no place else. From her stacks comes the soft breathing of her engines working in perfect unison; the gradual silencing and loss of vibration foretold the approach of shoaling water. A pilot who knew the boat could tell almost the exact depth of water under her bottom by the boat's feel that comes natural to a pilot. In later years with general use of condensers on steamers only the vibration of the boat told the story. Nothing was more cheerful on a cold winter night to the pilot than when the engineer scaped her out to reduce excess steam. Some steamers barked with a sharp pistol-like sound, or roared like a lion, and still others had a peculiar wheezy sigh, caused by worn cylinders and leaky rings. Yes, there was nothing so friendly on cold nights. Modern diesel boats are like automobiles, vibrationless [sic], purely a piece of marvelous compact power. Romance is gone from steamboating."

This is true, but romance is gone from many things in our culture, and we are the worse for its passing.

William Tippitt

In her anthology of riverboat stories, Curry awards Tippitt a prominent place. He grew up in Cairo, Illinois and spent much of his youth watching steamboats arrive at and depart from that city. Curry describes a knowledgeable man, full of gusto, mischievous, and cantankerous. "Tippitt worked in turn on the river, the railroad, and the newspaper for awhile before turning to the river for good. As a river reporter on the Cairo *Citizen* he wrote the [column] Shag Town River Ripples, under the pen name Huck Finn." He noted boat arrivals and departures, chitchat, scandals, and rumors. In 1924 Tippitt earned a first-class pilot's license "and piloted towboats, dredges, inspection vessels, and showboats." Along the way he gathered an enormous amount of information about steamers from which he prepared the compilation cited in this book. Tippitt retired in 1966, but never gave up his interest in steamboats. Though he crammed several occupations into his life, Tippitt admitted that "I had no intention of being anything but a steamboat pilot. I just couldn't get the river out of my blood."[159]

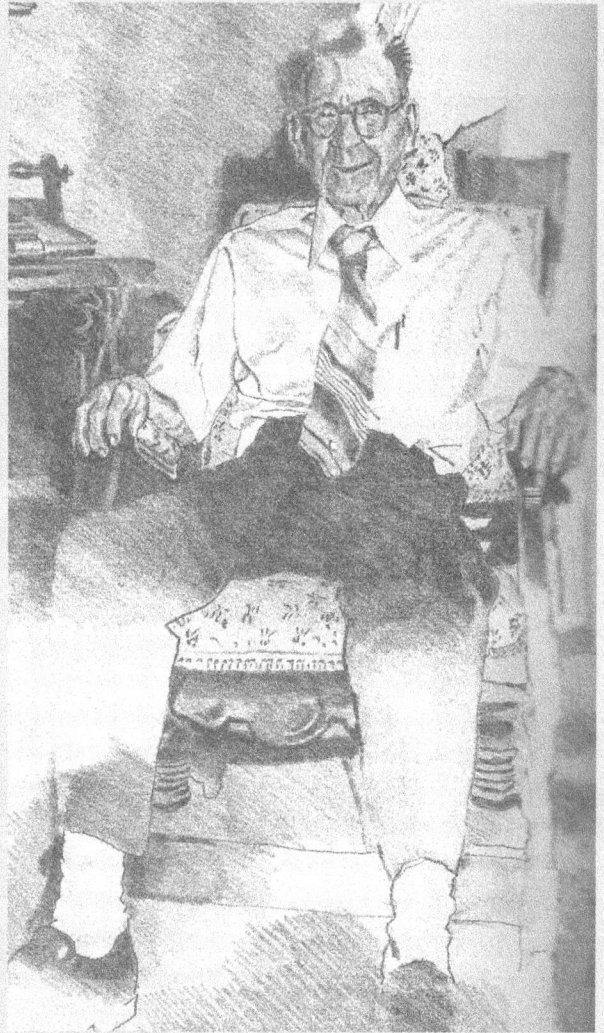

William Tippitt. Collection of Jane Curry.

[159]Curry, 161-162.

Selected Bibliography

Books:

Allsopp, Fred W., editor. *Folklore of Romantic Arkansas*, Vol. 2. New York: The Grollier Society, 1931.

Andrist, Ralph K. and C. Bradford Mitchell. *Steamboats on the Mississippi*. New York: American Heritage, 1962.

Audubon, Maria R. and Elliott Coues, editors. *Audubon and His Journals*, Vol. 1. New York: Scribner's Sons 1897.

Ayer, I. Winslow. *Life in the Wilds of America and Wonders of the West in and Beyond the Bounds of Civilization*. Grand Rapids: Central Publishing Company, 1880.

Bagnall, Norma Hayes. *On Shaky Ground: The New Madrid Earthquakes of 1811-1812*. Columbia: University of Missouri Press, 1996.

Baird, Robert. *View of the Valley of the Mississippi, or the Emigrant's and Traveler's Guide to the West*. Philadelphia: H. S. Tanner, 1834.

Baldwin, Leland D. *The Keelboat Age on Western Waters*. Pittsburgh: University of Pittsburgh Press, 1941.

Birkhau, Roy L. *The Great Steamboat Race*. Cincinnati: Young & Klein, 1962.

Bissell, Richard. *High Water*. Boston: Little, Brown and Company, 1954.

Blair, Walter A. *A Raft Pilot's Log*. Cleveland: Arthur H. Clark Company, 1930.

Bogart, E. L. and C. M. Thompson. *Readings in the Economic History of the United States*. New York: Longmans, Green and Co., 1916.

Bolton, S. Charles. *Arkansas, 1800-1860: Remote and Restless*. Fayetteville: University of Arkansas Press, 1998.

Botkin, B.A., editor. *A Treasury of Mississippi River Folklore*. New York: Bonanza Books, 1978.

Brennan, Stephen, editor. *An Autobiography of Davy Crockett*. New York: Skyhorse Publishing, 2011.

Buchanan, Thomas C. *Black Life on the Mississippi: Slaves, Free Blacks, and the Western Steamboat World*. Chapel Hill: University of North Carolina Press, 2004.

Burman, Ben Lucien. *Look Down that Winding River*. New York: Taplinger Publishing Company, 1973.

———— *Mississippi*. New York: Cosmopolitan Book Corporation, 1929.

Camillo, Charles and Matthew Pearcy. *Upon Their Shoulders: A History of the Mississippi River Commission from its Inception through the Advent of the Modern Mississippi River and Tributaries Project*. Vicksburg: Mississippi River Commission, 2004.

Capers, Gerald M., Jr. *The Biography of a River Town: Memphis: Its Heroic Age*. Chapel Hill: University of North Carolina Press, 1939.

Carter, Hodding. *Lower Mississippi*. New York: Farrar & Rhinehart, 1942.

Charnwood, Godfrey. *Abraham Lincoln. A Biography*. Lanham, Maryland: Madison Books, 1996 (Original published 1916).

Clement, William E. *Plantation Life on the Mississippi*. New Orleans: Pelican Publishing Co., 1953.

Curry, Jane. *The River's in My Blood. Riverboat Pilots Tell Their Stories*. Lincoln: University of Nebraska Press, 1983.

Daniel, Pete. *Deep'n As It Come: The 1927 Mississippi River Flood*. New York: Oxford University Press, 1977.

Danver, Steven L. and John R. Burch Jr., editors. *Encyclopedia of Water Politics and Policy in the United States*. Washington, D.C.: CQ-Press, 2011.

Davis, Helen, editor. *Trials of the Earth: The Autobiography of Mary Hamilton*. Jackson: University Press of Mississippi, 1992.

DeBlack, Thomas A. *With Fire and Sword, Arkansas, 1861-1874*. Fayetteville: University of Arkansas Press, 2003.

Dougan, Michael B. *Arkansas Odyssey. The Saga of Arkansas From Prehistoric Times to Present*. Little Rock: Rose Publishing Co., 1994.

Dougan, Michael B. and Carol W. Dougan. *By the Cypress Swamp*. Little Rock: Rose Publishing Co., 1980.

Devol, George H. *Forty Years a Gambler on the Mississippi*. Cincinnati, Ohio: Devol and Haines, 1887.

DeVoto, Bernard. *Mark Twain's America*. New York: Cambridge, 1951.

—————, ed. *"Old Times on the Mississippi." The Portable Mark Twain*. New York: Viking Press, 1968.

Dickens, Charles. *Pilgrim Edition of the Letters of Charles Dickens,* Vol. 3. London: Oxford University Press, 1988.

Dorsey, Florence L. *Master of the Mississippi, Henry Shreve and the Conquest of the Mississippi*. Boston: Houghton Mifflin Co., 1941.

Drago, Harry Sinclair. *The Steamboaters. From the Early Side-Wheelers to the Big Packets*. New York: Bramhall House, 1967.

Edrington, Mabel F. *History of Mississippi County, Arkansas* (Ocala, Florida: 1962.

Featherstonhaugh, G. W. *Excursion Through the Slave States*. New York: Harper and Brothers, 1844.

Field, Joseph M. "Stopping for Wood." *A Sampler of Old, Old Times on the Mississippi*. John Francis McDermott, editor. Carbondale: Southern Illinois University Press, 1968.

Ferguson, John and James H. Atkinson. *Historic Arkansas*. Little Rock: Arkansas History Commission, 1966.

Flint, Timothy. *Recollections of the Last Ten Years, Passed in Occasional Residences and Journeyings in the Valley of the Mississippi, from Pittsburgh and the Missouri to the Gulf of Mexico, and from Florida to the Spanish Frontier: In a series of Letters to the Rev. James Flint, of Salem, Massachusetts*. Boston: Cunnings, Hilliard, 1826.

Foti, Thomas. "The River's Gifts and Curses." *The Arkansas Delta, Land of Paradox*. Edited by Jeannie Whayne and Willard B. Gatewood. Fayetteville: University of Arkansas Press, 1993.

Gandy, Joan W. and Thomas H. *The Mississippi Steamboat Era in Historic Photographs, Natchez to New Orleans 1870-1920*. Mineola, New York: Dover Publications Inc., 1987.

Gould, E. W. *Fifty Years on the Mississippi or Gould's History of River Navigation*. Columbus, Ohio: Long's College Book Company, 1951.

Graham, Philip. *Showboats. The History of an American Institution*. Austin: University of Texas Press, 1951.

Greene, Francis Vinton. *Campaigns of the Civil War: The Mississippi*. Edison: New Jersey: Castle Books, 2002.

Gudmestad, Robert. *Steamboats and the Rise of the Cotton Kingdom*. Baton Rouge: Louisiana State University Press, 1964.

Heartstill, William W. *Fourteen Hundred and 91 Days in the Confdrat* [sic] *Army, A Journal Kept by W. W. Heartstill for Four Years, One Month, and One Day; or Camp Life; Day by Day, of the W. P. Lane Rangers, from April 9, 1861 to May 20, 1865*. Marshall, Texas, 1876.

Hempstead, Fay. *Historical Review of Arkansas*. Chicago: Lewis Publishing Co., 1911.

Holland, Robert A. *The Mississippi River in Maps and Views: From Lake Itasca to the Gulf of Mexico*. New York: Rizzoli, 2008.

Huddleston, Duane, Sammie Rose, and Pat Wood. *Steamboats and Ferries on White River: A Heritage Revisited*. Conway: University of Central Arkansas Press, 1998.

Huffman, Alan. *Sultana*. New York: Harper Collins, 2009.

Hunter, Louis C. *Steamboats on the Western Rivers: An Economic and Technological History*. New York: Dover Publications, 1949.

Jones, Mary Harris. *Autobiography of Mother Jones*. Mary Field Parton, ed. Chicago: Charles H. Kerr & Co., 1925.

Keith, Jeanette. *Fever Season. The story of the terrifying epidemic and the people who saved a city*. New York: Bloomsbury, 2012.

Latrobe, Charles Joseph. *The First Steamboat Voyage on the Western Waters.* Baltimore: John Murphy, Maryland Historical Society, 1871.

————. *The Rambler in North America*, Vol. 1. London: Seeley and Burnside, 1833.

Lloyd, James T. *Lloyd's Steamboat Directory and Disasters on the Western Waters.* Cincinnati: James T. Lloyd & Co., 1856.

Mackey, Robert R. *The Uncivil War. Irregular Warfare in the Upper South, 1861-1865.* Norman: University of Oklahoma Press, 2004.

Mahan, Alfred T. *The Gulf & Inland Waters.* New York: Blue & Gray Press, 1960.

McDermott, John Francis, editor. *Before Mark Twain: A Sampler of Old, Old Times on the Mississippi.* Carbondale: Southern Illinois University Press, 1968.

Melville Herman. *The Confidence Man: His Masquerade.* New York: Dix, 1857.

Milligan, John D. *Gunboats Down the Mississippi.* Annapolis: U. S. Naval Institute, 1965.

Morris, Wright, editor. *The Mississippi River Reader.* Garden City: Doubleday, 1962.

Nuttall, Thomas. *Journal of Travels into the Arkansas Territory During the Year 1818.* Philadelphia: Thomas H. Palmer Publisher, 1821.

Olmsted, Frederick Law. *The Cotton Kingdom: A Traveler's Observations on Cotton and Slavery in the American Slave States.* New York: Alfred A Knopf, 1953.

Pope, William F. *Early Days in Arkansas.* Little Rock: Frederick W. Allsop Publisher, 1895.

Porter, David Dixon. *The Naval History of the Civil War.* New York: The Sherman Publishing Co., 1886.

Potter, Jerry O. *Sultana Tragedy: America's Greatest Maritime Disaster.* Gretna, Louisisana: Pelican Publishing Co., 1992.

Pratt, Fletcher. *Civil War on Western Waters.* New York: Henry Holt, 1956.

Quick, Herbert and Edward Quick. *Mississippi Steamboatin'.* New York: Henry Holt and Company, 1926.

Raban, Jonathan. *Old Glory: A Voyage Down the Mississippi.* New York: Vintage, 1998.

Schneider, Paul. *Old Man River. The Mississippi River in North American History.* New York: Henry Holt and Company, 2013.

Steele Eliza. *A Summer Journey in the West.* New York: J. S. Tayler & Co., 1841,

Stewart-Abernathy, Leslie C., editor. *Ghost Boats on the Mississippi: Discovering Our Working Past.* Fayetteville: Arkansas Archeological Survey, University of Arkansas, 2002.

Thompson, George H. *Arkansas and Reconstruction.* Port Washington, N.Y.: Keennikat Press, 1976.

Twain, Mark. *Life on the Mississippi.* New York: Signet Classic, 2001.

Trollop, Frances. *Domestic Manners of the Americans.* New York: Alfred A. Knopf, 1904.

Ward, Geoffrey C., Dayton Duncan, and Ken Burns. *Mark Twain. An Illustrated Biography.* New York: Alfred A. Knopf, 2001.

Watkins, T. H. *Mark Twain's Mississippi.* Palo Alto: American West Publishing Company, 1974.

Way, Frederick. Jr. *Mississippi Stern-Wheelers.* Milwaukee: Kalmbach Publishing Company, 1947.

————. *She Takes the Horns: Steamboat Racing on the Western Waters.* Cincinnati: Young and Klein, 1953.

————. *Way's Packet Directory 1848-1994.* Athens: University of Ohio Press, revised edition, 1994.

Wayman, Norbury L. *Life on the River.* New York: Crown Publishers, Inc., 1971.

Weil, Tom. *The Mississippi River.* New York: Hippocrene Books, Inc., 1992.

Whayne, Jeannie and Willard B. Gatewood, editors. *The Arkansas Delta. Land of Paradox.* Fayetteville: University of Arkansas Press, 1993.

Whayne, Jeannie. Delta Empire. *Lee Wilson and the Transformation of Agriculture in the New South.* Baton Rouge: Louisiana State University Press, 2011.

Libraries:

A.B. Safford Library, Cairo, Illinois.

Arkansas State University Library, Jonesboro.

Carnegie Library, Pittsburgh, Pennsylvania.

Cossitt and Goodwyn Libraries, Memphis, Tennessee.

Inland Rivers Library, Public Library of Cincinnati and Hamilton County, Ohio.

Library of the University of Mississippi, Oxford.

Public Library, St. Louis, Missouri.

University of Arkansas Library, Fayetteville, Thomas E. Tappan Jr. Steamboat Collection.

Newspapers:

Arkansas *Advocate*

Arkansas Gazette

Arkansas Weekly Herald

Batesville *Guard*

Batesville *Weekly Record*

Baxter Bulletin

Des Arc *Citizen*

Fort Smith *Herald*

Jacksonport *Herald*

Louisville *Courier Journal*

Memphis *Appeal*

Memphis *Avalanche*

Memphis *Commercial Appeal*

Memphis *Scimitar*

Missouri Democrat

Missouri Republican

National Intelligencer

New Albany *Commercial*

New Orleans *Picayune*

New Orleans *Times*

Pittsburgh *Commercial*

Pittsburgh *Gazette*

Stars and Stripes

St. Louis *Daily Commercial Bulletin*

St. Louis *Republican*

Vicksburg *Herald*

West Memphis *Accelerator*

Periodicals:

Atkinson, James H. "Brooks Baxter Contest." *Arkansas Historical Quarterly* 4:2 (Summer 1945): 124-149.

Barnett, I. N. Sr. "Early Days of Batesville." *Arkansas Historical Quarterly* 11:1 (Spring 1952): 15-24.

Bearss, Edwin C. "The Battle of Helena, July 4, 1863." *Arkansas Historical Quarterly* 20:3 (Autumn 1961): 256-297.

Brown, Mattie. "River Transportation in Arkansas, 1819-1890." *Arkansas Historical Quarterly* 1:4 (September 1942): 342-354.

Brown, Sarah. "The Arkansas Traveler: Southwest Humor on Canvas." *Arkansas Historical Quarterly* 46:4 (Winter 1987): 348-375.

Burghardt, Andrew. "The Location of River Towns in the Central Lowland of the United States." *Annals of the Association of American Geographers* 49 (September 1959): 305-323.

Carter, Deane G. "A Place in History for Ann James." *Arkansas Historical Quarterly* 28:4 (Winter 1969): 309-321.

Driggs, Orval Truman Jr. "The Issues of the Powell Clayton Regime." *Arkansas Historical Quarterly* 8:1 (Spring 1949): 1-75.

Fair, James R. "Hopefield, Arkansas: Important River-Rail Terminal." *Arkansas Historical Quarterly* 57:2 (Summer 1998): 191-204.

Herndon, Dallas T. "A Little of What Arkansas Was Like a Hundred Years Ago." *Arkansas Historical Quarterly* 3:2 (Summer 1944): 97-124.

Hodges, Dr. T. L. "Possibilities for the Archeologist and Historian in Eastern Arkansas." *Arkansas Historical Quarterly* 2:2 (June 1943): 141-163.

Holder, Virgil H. "Historical Geography of the Lower White River." *Arkansas Historical Quarterly* 27:2 (Summer 1968):132-145.

Holmes, William F. "The Arkansas Cotton Pickers Strike of 1891." *Arkansas Historical Quarterly* 32:2 (Summer 1973): 107-119.

Howell, Elmo. "Mark Twain's Arkansas." *Arkansas Historical Quarterly* 29:3 (Autumn 1970): 195-208.

Huff, Leo E. "Guerillas, Jayhawkers and Bushwhackers in Northern Arkansas During the Civil War." *Arkansas Historical Quarterly* 24:2 (Summer 1965): 127-148.

—————. "The Military Board of Confederate Arkansas." *Arkansas Historical Quarterly* 26:1 (Spring 1967): 75-95.

Jones, Irene. "Hot Springs: Ante-Bellum Watering Place." *Arkansas Historical Quarterly* 14:1 (Spring 1955): 3-31.

Keeler, Ralph, and Alfred R. Waud. "From Vicksburg to Memphis, With Some Account of an Explosion." *Every Saturday* 3 (August 19, 1871): 284-285.

Kingsbury, Cyrus. "Journal of the Mission Among the Cherokees of Arkansas." *Missionary Herald* 17 (May 30, 1820): 149.

Long, Stephen H. "Extent of Steam Navigation on the Western Waters." *Journal of the Franklin Institute* 15 (May 1848): 354-355.

Lyon, Owen. The Quapaws and Little Rock." *Arkansas Historical Quarterly* 8:4 (Winter 1949): 336-342.

Moffatt, Walter. "Transportation in Arkansas, 1819-1840." *Arkansas Historical Quarterly* 15:3 (Autumn 1956): 195.

Morris, Robert L. "Three Arkansas Travelers." *Arkansas Historical Quarterly* 4:3 (Autumn 1945): 215-230.

Richards, Ira Don. "The Battle of Poison Spring." *Arkansas Historical Quarterly* 8:4 (Winter 1959): 338-349.

—————. "Little Rock on the Road to Reunion, 1865-1880." *Arkansas Historical Quarterly* 25:4 (Winter 1966): 312-335.

Ross, Margaret Smith. "Nathan Warren, a Free Negro of the Old South." *Arkansas Historical Quarterly* 15:1 (Spring 1956): 53-61.

Sherwood, Diana. "Clearing The Channel-The Snagboat in Arkansas." *Arkansas Historical Quarterly* 3:1 (Spring 1944):53-62.

Tedford, Harold C. "Circuses in Northwest Arkansas Before the Civil War." *Arkansas Historical Quarterly* 26:3 (Autumn 1967): 244-256.

Wall, Effie Allison. "Early Boating on St. Francis and Interesting Reminiscences As Told By Mrs. Margaret Clark." *Arkansas Historical Quarterly* 7:3 (Autumn 1948): 227-230.

Walz, Robert B. "Migration Into Arkansas, 1820-1880: Incentives and Means of Travel." *Arkansas Historical Quarterly* 17:4 (Winter 1958): 309-324.

West, Mabel. "Jacksonport, Arkansas: Its Rise and Decline." *Arkansas Historical Quarterly* 9:4 (Winter 1950): 231-258.

White, Lonnie J. "Some Old French Place Names in the State of Arkansas." *Arkansas Historical Quarterly* 19:3 (Autumn 1960): 191-206.

Wood, Stephen E. "The Development of Arkansas Railroads." *Arkansas Historical Quarterly* 7:2 (Summer 1948): 103-140.

Worley, Ted R. "Glimpses of an Old Southwest Town." *Arkansas Historical Quarterly* 8:2 (Summer 1949): 133-159.

—————. "Early Days in Osceola." *Arkansas Historical Quarterly* 24:2 (Summer 1965): 120-126.

—————. "Helena on the Mississippi." *Arkansas Historical Quarterly* 12:1 (Spring 1954): 1-15.

—————. "Bypaths of Arkansas History." *Arkansas Historical Quarterly* 12:4 (Winter 1953): 394-398.

—————, ed. "Diary of Lieutenant Orville Gillet, U. S. A., 1864-1865." *Arkansas Historical Quarterly* 17:2 (Summer 1968): 164-204.

Reports

Survey for Submerged Cultural and Natural
Resources, White River Navigation Project.
Final Report Vol. I. April 2001. By Michael
Krivor and Andrew Buchner, Panamerican
Consultants, Inc., Memphis, Tennessee.

Survey for Submerged Cultural and Natural
Resources, White River Navigation
Maintenance, Arkansas, Desha, and Prairie
Counties, Arkansas. Final Report Vol. II. May
2004. By Charles E. Pearson, Coastal
Environments, Inc. Baton Rouge, Louisiana
and Michael Tuttle and Michael Krivor,
Panamerican Consultants, Inc. Memphis,
Tennessee.

Typescripts

Steamboats, 1870-1872, Vol. 1. Typescript on file,
Helena, Arkansas Public Library.

Steamboats, 1873-1876, Vol. 2. Typescript on file,
Helena, Arkansas Public Library.

Steamboats, 1877-1879, Vol. 3. Typescript on file,
Helena, Arkansas Public Library.

Appendix A: Tippit Compilation of Hulks on the Lower Mississippi River.

From Island No. 1 to Island No. 8: *Bluff City, Clinton, Commodore Perry, Dan Able, Hickman, John Gault, Lady of the Lake, Louisiana, Mary Clifton, Nashville, Potesi, Ruth,* and *Sultan.*

Vicinity of Island No. 10: *A. D. Crossman, Chillicothe, Enterprise, Fred Tern, John J. Roe, John Simons, Winchester,* and *Yazoo.*

Below Island No. 10: *Alaska, Archimide, Brilliant, Dresden, General Robertson, General Scott, Hudson, Missouri, New York, Tuscahoma,* and *Walnut Hill.*

In Echles Bend: *Colonel Dickinson, Cooga, Farmer, Governor Dodge, Havana, J. D. Perry, Linwood, Lon Stickney, Oceans, Sunnyside, T. Lacy, Tycoon,* and *Virginia.*

In Island No. 21 Bend: *H. D. Newcomb, Relia, Smithland,* and *Storm.*

At foot of Island No. 21: *76, Belle, Elba, Gould,* and *St. Charles.*

At Island No. 26: *Caspian, Daniel Boone, Henry Bry, Kate Aubrey, Magic,* and *Orb.*

In Plumb Point Bend: *America, Carolina, Elisa, Empire State, Eugene, Illinois, Jubilee, Neptune, Oregon, St. Cloud, Telegraph, Tom Corwin,* and *Yankee.*

At Island No. 34: *Argo, Empress, Henry Clay, Niagara,* and *Vulcan.*

In Island No. 35 chute: *Emma No. 3.*

In Devil's Race Grounds: *Alhambra, Brandywine, Pacific, Silver Spray, South Bend,* and *St. Mary.*

At Island No. 40: *Fannie Brandeis, Sultana, Tuscambia,* and *W.R. Arthur.*

Paddy Hen and Chickens: *A. L. Shotwell.*

Memphis and vicinity: *Attakapas, Belle of Pike, Champion, Constitution, Excelsior, General Lovell, George Collier, Mayflower, Ned Barker, Ned Jones, R. P. Walt, St. Francis,* and *St. Patrick.*

President's Island and below: *Adelaide, Beauregard, Belle of Clarksville, Belle of Natchez, City of Memphis, Courtland, Crescent City, Delaware, DeWitt Clinton, Diligent, Favorite, Florence, General Ben, Gulnare, James Madison, Jeff Thompson, Jennie Brown, Little Alps, Little Pike, Lucy Holcomb, Madison, Mariner, Massachusetts, Montezuma, Niagara, Olive Branch, Pennsylvania, Platte Valley, R. F. Sass, R. H. Lockwood, Rowena, Saline, St. Nicholas, T .L. McGill, Tom Jefferson, Undine, Webster,* and *Westerner.*

Island No. 66 and below: *Allen Collier, Avendale, Countess, Decatur, Defender, Dick Vernon, Dunleith, Julia, Justice, Maggie Hays, Martha, Mohawk, Selma, V. P. Wilson,* and *Washington.*

Scrubgrass and vicinity: *Lizzie Gill.*

Vicinity of White River: *Belle Zane, Clarksville, Forest Rose, Hector, Humboldt, Kate French, Rainbow,* and *Savannah.*

Vicinity of Island No. 76: *Amazon, Chiefton, Dr. Watson, Kate Joyes, Matamora, Monarch, Norma,* and *Pocahontas.*

In Yellow Bend and below: *B. M. Runyen, California, Clarksville, David White, Fanny Bullitt, Garden City, General Pike, H. S. Day, John Adams, John Strader, Kate Kearney, Leopard, Minnesota, Oregon, St. Joseph,* and *Webster.*

Grand Lake vicinity: *Ben Franklin, Clara, Congress, Daniel O'Connell, Nick Walt, Sam Gaty, Tarquin,* and *Western World.*

Island 93 vicinity: *Belfast, Bulletin, Daniel Boone, Return,* and *Tennessee.*

Near New Brunswick: *Agnes, Brunswick, City of Madison, Cora Anderson, Henry Clay, Judah Truro, Nebraska, Nick Biddle, Switzerland, Tigress, W. R. Campbell, W. R. Carter, Western,* and *Wyandotte.*

In Palmira's Bend: *Adriatic, Ganges, Hero, Huron, Joseph Pierce, Midiator, Montgomery,* and *Telegraph.*

At Grand Gulf: *Conestoga, George Washington, Horizon, St. Louis,* and *Star.*

In Rodney Reach: *Convoy, Express, Henry Ames, Mary Agnes, Mississippi, Monroe, Pathfinder, Prairie Belle, William T. Berry,* and *Woodman.*

Appendix B: List of Boats Included

Acacia

Acacia Cottage

Adams

Ad. Hine

Admiral

Agnes

A.H. Sevier

AID

A.J. White

Alberta

Alberta No. 2

Alberta No. 3

Albert Pearce

Alleghany

Alps

Altoona

American/America

Amulet

Andy Baum

A.R. Bragg

Archie P. Green

Archimedes

Argonaut No. 2

Argos

Argosy

Arkadelphia City

Arkansas

Arkansas (ram)

Arkansas Belle

Arkansas City

Arkansas Traveler

Arlington

Ashland

Austin Corbin

A. W. Quarrier

Banjo

Batesville

Bayou Boeuf

B.B.

Bedford

Belle Lee

Belle of Pike

Belle of Texas

Belle Peoria

Belle St. Louis

Belle Zane

Ben Wood

Birdie Bailey

Black Hawk

Bluella

Blue Wing

Blue Wing No. 2

Bluff City

B.M. Runyan

Bob Hardy

Border City

Bracelet

Bridge City

Buckeye State

Bulletin

Business

Buzzard

Caddo

Cambridge

Camden

Canton

Capitol City

Caroline

Carondelet

Carrie S. Douglas

Carrie V. Kountz

Catahoula

Catawba

C. B. Reese

Cedar Rapids

Celeste

Centralia

Chapmans Theatre

Charm

Chas. Bodeman

Chas. P. Choteau

Cherokee

Chester Ashley

Chickasaw

Chicot

Chippewa

Choctaw

Cincinnati

City of Alton

City of Augusta

City of Chester

City of Forsyth

City of Helena

City of Idaho

City of Little Rock

City of Quincy

Clara Bell

Clara L

Clermont

Clermont No. 2

C.N. Craft

Colossal

Comet

Commercial

Conestoga

Conway

Cora Belle

Cotton Plant

Covington

Covington No. 2

C. R. Cummings

Creole

Crescent City

Cricket

Curlew

Dan Rice's Floating Opera
    House Museum

Dardanelle

Davenport

David Tatum

Dean Adams

Defender

De Kalb

Delta

Des Arc

De Smet

DeSoto

D. H. Morton

Diligent

Dispatch

Diurnal

Dr. Buffington

Duck

Eagle

Eclipse

Economist

Ed Richardson

Edinburgh

Editor

Edward J. Gay

Eliza Fox

Eliza G.

Ella

Ella Hecht

Elva

Elwood

Emma

Emma No. 2

Emma No. 3

Emma C. Elliott

E.M. Ryland

Era No. 6

Eugene

Exporter

Fair Play

Fairy Queen

Fannie Tatum

Fanny Moore

Fanny Ogden

Fawn

Florence

Florence Meyer

Florence Miller No. 2

Florence Traber

Forest City

Forest Queen

Forest Rose

Fort Gibson

Fort Gibson No. 2

Fort Smith

Four Boys

Fox

Frederic Notrebe

Freddie

Freddy Robinson

Frontier City

F.W. Tucker

General Anderson

General Bem

General Bragg

General Brown

General Charles H. Tompkins

General Jeff Thompson

General Lane

General Pierson

General Pike

General Price

General P.T. Beauregard

General Shields

George, C. Wolff

George W. Decker

Georgia Lee

G.H. Van Etten

Gladiator

Glasgow

Glide

Glide No. 3

G.M. Sively

Goldena

Golden State

Gov. Allen

Governor Bent

Governor Garland

Grampus No. 2

Grand Republic

Grand Tower

Granger

Grapeshot

Gray Eagle

Great Republic

Grosse Tete

Guidon

Gulnare

Gunboat No. 25

G.W. Cheek

G. W. Lyons

G. W. Mayo

Hallie

Harp

Hastings

Hattie B. Nowland

H.D. Mears

Hector

Helen Brooks

Heliopolis

Henry C. Yaegar

Henry Sheldon

Hercules

Hesper

Hickman

Highland Laddie

Hinds

Holston

I Go

Illinois

Indiana

Interchange

Irene

Irma

Iron City

Isaac Shelby

Jacob Musselman

Jack Porter

James Laughllin

James Lee

James Raymond

J.A. Woodson

J. B. Gordon

J.B. Woods

Jefferson

Jeff Thomson

Jennie Howell

Jennie May

Jesse Lazear

J.F. Joy

J. H. Done

J. H. Miller

J. J. Cadot

J. Morrisett

J. M. White

Joe Peters

Joe Wilson

John Howard

John Matthews

John M. Chambers
John B. Maud
John Briggs
John D. Perry
John Means
John Overton
John Porter,
John R. Meigs
Josie
Josie D. Harkins
Josie Harry
J.S. Dunham
J.S. McCune
Julia
Julia Dean
Julia Roane
Kanawha Valley No. 2
Kate Adams
Kate Bruner
Kate Hart
Katie
Katie Hooper
Katie Morrison
Katie P. Kountz
Katydid
Kenton
Kentuckian
Kentucky
Key West
L. E. Patton
Lady
Lady Boone
Lady Jackson
Laura
Laurel
Legal Tender
Lelia
Leni Leoti
Leon
Leonidas
Lew Preston
Lexington
Liberty
Liberty No. 2
Lightwood
Lilly Martin

Linden
Linnie Drown
Linton
Little Rock
Lizzie Gill
Lizzie Simmons
Lorna Doone
Louisa
Louise Stetcher
Louisville
Low Water
Luella
Luella Brown
Luminary
Maggie Hays
Maid of Peru
Market Boy
Mark Twain
Marlen Speed
Mary Bell
Mary Boyd
Mary Elizabeth
Mary E. Poe
Mary F. Carter
Mary L. Dougherty
Mary Patterson
Mason
Mattie
Maumelle
Maurepas
May Duke
May Flower
May Queen
McArthur
Memphis
Mercury
Miami
Milt Harry
Milton Brown
Minnie
Molly Hamilton
Monarch
Monmouth
Monsoon
Moselle
Mound City

Mount Vernon
M.S. Mepham
Music
Myrtle
Natchez
Natoma
Natrona
Naumkeag
Nellie Thomas
Neosho
New Mary Morgan
New Mattie
New Moon
New National
New Orleans
New Sensations
Niagara
Nick Longworth
Nick of the Woods
Nightingale
North Missouri
Octavia
Ohio Bell
Only Chance
Ora Lee
Orlando
Osage
Osceola
Osceola Belle
Ottawa
Ozark Queen
Pat Cleburne
Peerless
Persian
Petrolia
Petrolia No. 2
Phil Allin
Philip Pennywitt
Picayune
Pike
Pine Bluff
Pink Varble
Pitser Miller
Platte Valley
Pocahontas
Pontchartrain

Pontiac

Post Boy

Prairie

Prairie State

Princess

Progress

Quapaw

Queen

Queen City

Quickstep

Rainbow

Ralph

Randall

Rattler

R. C. Gray

Rebecca

Red Rover

Red Wing

Reindeer

Rene Macready

Return

Revenue

R.F. Sass

Rhoad

Rhoda

Ringgold

Robert E. Lee

Robert Hardy

Robert Thompson

Rob Roy

Rock City

Rodolph

Rolla

Romeo

Rosa Bland

Rosa Miller

Rose City

Rose Hambleton

Roseville

Rough and Ready

Rowena

R. P. Converse

R. P. Walt

Russ Porter

Ruth

Sallie

Sallie Anderson

Sam Hale

Sam Ham

Sangamon

Santa Fe

S. C. Day

Seminole

S. H. Tucker

Sidney Dillon

Silver Wave

Sioux City

Sovereign

S. P. Pond

St. Cloud

Steubenville

St Francis (Nos. 1-3)

St. Francis Belle

St. Francis Trader

S. Thayer

St. Joseph

St. Louis

St. Marys

Stonewall

Sultana

Summer Coon

Sunbeam

Sunny South

Superior

Swain

Tahlequah

Tallatchie

T. B. Allen

Tecumseh

Tempest

Tennessean

T.F. Eckert

35th Parallel

Thomas B. Florence

Thomas, H. Allen

Thomas Jefferson

Thomas P. Ray

Tinclad No. 34

Tippecanoe

T. L. McGill

T. N. Cligg

Trader

Tremont

Trenton

Tuscaroras

Tycoon

Tyler

Umpire No. 2

Undine

Utah

Van Buren

Velocipede

Victoria

Victory

Violet

Virginia

Volant

Wabash Valley

W. A. Caldwell

W. A King

Walt Allen

War Eagle

Warner

Warren

Washington

Waverly

W. Butler

Welcome

West Wind

Wheeling

White Cliff

White National

White Water

W. H. Langley

Wichita

William Armstrong

William Hurlbert

William Parsons

William Purson

William Wallace

Will Kyle

Winnie

Wm. Druhe No. 2

Yachita

Yazoo

Yellow Hecher

Zip McCoy

Edward J. Gay, in operation from 1878 to 1888, drew people from miles around, thanks to a melodious whistle that earned for it the nickname "mocking bird." Familiar scenes such as this along Mississippi River landings began fading into history by the turn of the twentieth century.   Steamboat Times.